Positive Behavior Interventions and Supports for Preschool and Kindergarten

Positive Behavior Interventions *and* Supports

FOR PRESCHOOL AND KINDERGARTEN

MARLA J. LOHMANN, PHD

Redleaf Press®
www.redleafpress.org
800-423-8309

Published by Redleaf Press
10 Yorkton Court
St. Paul, MN 55117
www.redleafpress.org

First edition 2021
Cover design by Danielle Carnito
Cover photograph by Monkey Business/Adobe Stock
Interior design by Douglas Schmitz
Typeset in Adobe Garamond
Printed in the United States of America
28 27 26 25 24 23 22 21   1 2 3 4 5 6 7 8

Library of Congress Cataloging-in-Publication Data

Names: Lohmann, Marla J., author.
Title: Positive behavior interventions and supports for preschool and
    kindergarten / by Marla J. Lohmann.
Description: First edition. | St. Paul, MN : Redleaf Press, 2021. |
    Includes bibliographical references and index. | Summary: "Positive
    Behavior Interventions & Supports (PBIS) is an evidence-based framework
    for preventing and addressing challenging behaviors in the classroom; it
    has shown to be effective from preschool through high school. Positive
    Behavior Interventions and Supports for Preschool and Kindergarten will
    provide specific information for preschool and kindergarten teachers on
    creating and implementing a classroom-wide behavior management system,
    as well as research-based interventions for addressing challenging
    behaviors"— Provided by publisher.
Identifiers: LCCN 2021005044 (print) | LCCN 2021005045 (ebook) | ISBN
    9781605546841 (paperback) | ISBN 9781605546858 (ebook)
Subjects: LCSH: Behavior modification. | Behavioral assessment of children.
    | Preschool children--Psychology. | Teacher-student relationships. |
    Classroom management.
Classification: LCC LB1060.2 .L65 2021 (print) | LCC LB1060.2 (ebook) |
    DDC 370.15/28--dc23
LC record available at https://lccn.loc.gov/2021005044
LC ebook record available at https://lccn.loc.gov/2021005045

Printed on acid-free paper

This book is dedicated to all of the preschool and kindergarten teachers who get up every day and do one of the most important jobs in the world. Thank you for your never-ending passion and dedication to children and families. The world is a better place because of you!

Contents

Acknowledgments

I would like to thank the people who have supported me in this book-writing journey. Without each one of you, this book would never have been completed.

First, I would like to thank my family. Abigail, Charlotte, Esther, and Abraham—you provide me with countless opportunities to practice what I teach in terms of addressing challenging and undesired behaviors. You also remind me every day why I do what I do. Thank you for that! Thank you, Mark, for supporting me and for not saying that I was crazy to take on this book project with four little kids and a full-time job! I am so thankful to be your partner in this crazy life. I love you all so much!

In addition, I would like to thank the colleagues who have helped grow me as a teacher and teacher educator. Thank you to Drs. Lyndal Bullock, Kathy Boothe, Brittany Hott, Ruby Owiny, Jen Walker, Kathy Randolph, Ariane Gauvreau, Kate Hovey, Johanna Higgins, Wendy Wendover, Bush White, Jeff Renfrow, John Murray, and Ms. Kathy Johnson. Each of you has challenged me to think critically about the field of education and supported me with words of encouragement in this process. Without your support, feedback, and guidance, I would not be where I am today and this book would never have been written.

Next I want to thank my Colorado Christian University special education teacher candidates. Thank you for working so hard to support children and families. Your passion, dedication, and hard work motivate me to be a better teacher. You are the reason that I do what I do, and you are the reason I have the best job in the world! Thank you!

Finally, I want to thank the amazing editors at Redleaf Press. Lindsey—I want to thank you for taking a chance on me and supporting my dream to write a book. Heidi—thank you for your patience, guidance, and knowledge when I was writing the first draft. And Melissa—I have loved working with you and am so glad that I got to finish this process with you. Your feedback has been invaluable and you have made me a better writer. Thanks for being my editor!

A Letter from the Author

Dear Readers,

As I am finishing writing this book, it is Janurary 2021. The past year has brought countless changes to your classrooms and a level of uncertainty as you plan for the future. I want to thank you for rising to the challenges that have appeared and those that continue to surface. Your hard work during this time is going to have an impact that will last for lifetimes—thank you for this!

COVID-19 resulted in many of you learning to support children's learning and development remotely, while also caring for the health needs of yourselves and your families. The economic impact of COVID has had numerous effects on children, including lost homes, food instability, child abuse, grief, and mental health concerns. The Black Lives Matter movement has brought an increased awareness to our communities of the racial injustices that have occurred in our history and continue to occur on a daily basis. The events in Washington, DC, on January 6, 2021, highlighted the division and injustices that exist in our nation. In addition, natural disasters such as wildfires and hurricanes have displaced families for extended periods of time. Each of these events has a direct impact on the children in your classrooms and their families, and in the coming years many children will be experiencing some level of trauma related to current national and world events.

I want to reassure you that the Positive Behavior Interventions and Supports (PBIS) framework is not only appropriate but ideal for supporting young children through these times. The components of PBIS Tier 1 include trauma-informed practices, such as a focus on relationships with children and families, collaborative teaming, and explicit instruction regarding expectations. These evidence-based practices will help to make your classroom a safe place for children, even in the midst of chaos in their homes and communities. Through implementing PBIS, you can create a place that is socially, emotionally, physically, and mentally safe for all children.

As you navigate the uncertain waters of the coming years, please know that I am thinking of you and of your students. Thank you again for the amazing work you are doing for children!

—Marla

CHAPTER 1

Challenging Behaviors in the Preschool Setting: An Overview

It's Monday morning in Miss Smith's preschool classroom, and the children are enjoying choice time in the learning centers. Suzie and Billy have been playing together in the block center for about fifteen minutes with no problems, but suddenly Miss Smith hears Suzie scream. She rushes to the block center to find Suzie on the floor with Billy on top of her, hitting her in the head with a block. Miss Smith picks up Billy and rushes him to the preschool director's office; he is sent home for the day. The next day, Billy returns to school and the same scenario happens again.

Events such as this one occur daily in preschool and kindergarten classrooms. Children misbehave, and teachers must respond. Some misbehaviors are small, like not flushing the toilet. Other behaviors, like biting and kicking, harm other children. But all challenging behaviors have the potential to be detrimental to learning and development. Ultimately, teachers need to address all inappropriate behaviors that happen in the classroom.

Preschool and kindergarten teachers face student behaviors such as:

lack of self-control,

difficulty cooperating with peers,

lack of attention and hyperactivity,

noncompliance and opposition,

physical aggression,

verbal aggression, and

other externalizing behaviors. (Baillargeon et al. 2007; Peckham-Hardin 2002; Tobin and Sugai 2005; Webster-Stratton and Hammond 1998)

A 2006 article by Gilliam and Shahar suggests that almost 40 percent of preschool teachers have suspended a student for behavioral challenges; this is thirteen times higher than the national suspension rate for K–12 students. Nearly a decade later, Gilliam reaffirmed that nothing had improved (Gilliam 2014).

At the beginning of this chapter, you read about Miss Smith, Billy, and Suzie. The situation in their classroom is not uncommon, and it is the reason I wrote this book. Challenging behaviors are normal, they occur in every classroom, and many are developmentally appropriate. However, that does not make them easy to manage. Luckily, you have decided to read this book to increase your ability to manage the challenging behaviors using Positive Behavior Interventions and Supports (PBIS), which is an evidence-based approach to guiding and supporting children's behavior. PBIS includes three tiers of support to ensure that the needs of all children are met. In the first PBIS tier, teachers provide a foundation for children's development and use proactive instruction paired with explicit feedback to teach all children the classroom expectations. In the second tier, teachers offer additional instruction interventions to aid young children who exhibit challenging behaviors. The third tier is used when young children need individualized instruction and interventions designed to address specific challenging behaviors that persist even with Tiers 1 and 2 supports.

As you read on, you will find that each chapter has specific tasks for you to complete. Many of the things I will ask you to do will take some time. You cannot implement a quality PBIS program (or, frankly, any program) without considerable time and dedication. Expect the process of implementing the PBIS framework to take you a minimum of several weeks but possibly several months. While you may feel excited and want to do it all immediately, please take the time to implement the suggestions and work through the activities presented here. A few months from now, you will be thankful that you took the time to do it right.

As you prepare to read this book and to do the hard work of implementing PBIS, I want to remind you why this is worth your time. In the short term, fewer behavior problems will make teaching easier and increase children's learning in your classroom. But, more important, providing young children with the knowledge and skills to meet the behavioral expectations in your classroom will set them up for success as they enter new environments later in their lives. The primary reason we use PBIS (and why I love it so much) is that it is not about forcing children to comply with our demands or making our lives easier. Instead, it is about teaching skills and reinforcing appropriate choices. Ultimately, our goal as we address challenging behaviors in preschool is to set children up for success as they grow. Knowing that the hard work you are doing today will have a lifelong impact is pretty awesome.

In addition, I want to help frame how you think about behavior. Too often we talk about behavior as a "problem." I sometimes hear the words "bad kid" used in reference to a child with inappropriate behaviors. But I want to challenge you to think about behavior a little differently. Behavior is a skill to be learned, and your job as a teacher is to guide that learning. I would venture to guess that it does not upset you when a child comes to your classroom unable to read—you know that learning to read is a skill that will develop over time with the right instruction, and it won't happen until the child is developmentally ready. The truth is that appropriate behavior is very similar. Socially acceptable behavior is a skill to be learned, and instruction on behaviors must be developmentally appropriate. Your job is to teach behavior, just like you teach other school readiness skills.

CHAPTER OVERVIEWS

As you begin to read this book, I want to provide you with a short overview of the chapters. The book begins with basic information about PBIS and then moves to specific recommendations for implementing it at each of the three levels. Many of the chapters provide specific examples of how the information may be put into practice, as well as offering sample planning and data collection forms. In the appendixes section, you will find blank copies of each of the forms to fill out as you complete the steps of the PBIS process. You may access a downloadable version of each of these forms via the QR codes in the appendixes.

Chapter 2 provides an overview of the PBIS process and some basic information that will support you as you begin to carry it out. In this chapter, you will begin planning how you will use the PBIS framework in your classroom. Because a solid plan is necessary for success, you should expect that it will take you at least a few weeks to get through chapter 2. I strongly urge you not to rush the process, as better plans will lead to better results.

In chapter 3, I introduce you to the practices that should be constantly occurring in your classroom and implemented at all levels of PBIS. These practices include respecting each child, respecting the cultures represented in your classroom, following evidence-based practices, and using action-research to guide instructional decisions. As you look at this list of practices, you are likely thinking that you already do these things. The reality is that a good PBIS framework is built upon good teaching practices, so yes, you are likely doing many of the things I recommend in Tier 1.

Chapter 4 presents the first Tier 1 PBIS practice: collaboration with families. In this chapter, I explain why working with families is critical and why building solid relationships with families is an important part of your job as a teacher. In addition, I present a variety of ways that you can build strong relationships with the families in your classroom and offer ideas for encouraging collaboration amid a variety of barriers.

Chapter 5 presents the second Tier 1 PBIS practice: building relationships with students. The research clearly tells us that children are more likely to succeed when they have a strong relationship with their teacher and with other adults in their lives. But building that relationship can be easier said than done, especially when a child shows challenging behaviors. This chapter provides practical strategies for connecting with all of the children in your classroom.

Chapter 6 is the longest chapter in the book, but it is my favorite chapter to work through. This chapter presents the Tier 1 practice of designing and teaching classroom expectations and routines. Expect to spend some time completing the work in this chapter, but when you are done, I am confident that you will be even more excited about the upcoming changes in your classroom!

Chapter 7 bridges beyond Tier 1 with a final prevention strategy before making interventions—effective instruction. Sometimes we can change children's challenging behaviors simply by changing the way we teach. Matching our instruction to the learning needs of children prevents many problematic behaviors. This chapter talks about how to identify and address a mismatch between teaching and learning.

In chapter 8, we dig into individual student behaviors and talk about the reasons children (and adults) misbehave. All behaviors, positive and negative, have a function, and effective behavior management requires you to determine the purpose of the behavior. The activities in chapter 8 will help you to identify why the children in your classroom are having a hard time with their behavior.

Chapter 9 will help as you design a behavior plan to meet the unique needs of a particular child or a group of children. In this chapter, I talk about choosing interventions and using very simple data to determine whether our interventions are working.

Chapter 10 focuses on supporting young children with challenging behaviors by implementing Tier 2 interventions. These interventions include removal of the problem-causing item, time-out from the activity, redirection/distraction, nonverbal cues, visual reminders and cues, provision of choices, behavior-specific praise, and pre-correction statements. This chapter provides specific instructions for using each of these interventions in the preschool or kindergarten classroom.

Chapter 11 offers the basic knowledge you will need to support the social-emotional needs of children with the most challenging behaviors. Some children will require one-on-one individualized supports to meet your classroom behavior expectations. This chapter will give you the knowledge and skills to provide that support to children in your classroom through Tier 3 interventions. The specific interventions discussed in this chapter include teaching new skills, teaching replacement behaviors, and offering structured breaks, individualized visual cues, rewards, behavior contracts, and sensory tools.

The conclusion wraps up the preceding chapters with a brief review of PBIS. In addition, I supply you with additional resources that may support you in your preschool or kindergarten PBIS journey.

Next I provide a discussion guide for teacher teams that are using this book together. If possible, I recommend trying PBIS with at least one other person. You will be more successful if you can encourage one another and help each other celebrate the wins. The questions in the discussion guide are simple and are meant to get you thinking and talking.

The book concludes with an appendix of forms you can use as you implement PBIS. You may notice that the forms are very basic—you might even describe them as boring. I did this for three reasons. Simple forms help you focus on what is truly important so that you will not be distracted by graphics or information that will take your focus away from the point of the activity. Second, boring forms are uninteresting to children, and they will be unlikely to want to look at your paper more than once. And finally, black-and-white images and text make this book more affordable for you. (If you would like the forms to be more visually appealing, I recommend copying them on colored paper or using stickers to decorate them.) Personalize them to meet your needs, but be sure that anything you do does not detract from the focus of the form.

MOVING FORWARD

As you read through this book, you will notice that my writing is often informal. Like any good preschool teacher, I have a vivid imagination, and I like to pretend that you and I are sitting down to a cup of coffee and talking through PBIS together. I believe it is easier for me to explain the concepts of PBIS and for you to fully grasp them when we chat like friends. And because we are friends now, let me tell you a bit about me. I started my career in a community child care center in Houston before becoming a K–8 special education teacher in both Houston and Chicago. I loved my years in the classroom and think teachers are the greatest group of people in the universe, so I love that I get to prepare people to be teachers now in my job as a university professor. In addition to my career in the field of education, I am the mother of four children between the ages of five and twelve, so I get to practice my behavior management skills countless times every day.

So, pour yourself a large cup of coffee, grab a handful of M&M's, and pull up a chair. Let's get started. I am so excited to have coffee with you and chat about my favorite topic: teaching young children and supporting their growth and development.

CHAPTER 2

Overview of PBIS

Mr. Juarez teaches kindergarten in a local public school. It is his third year in the classroom, but he is thinking of changing careers once the school year ends. The constant behavioral issues are just too much; they make him physically weary and keep him up at night. On a daily basis, he deals with temper tantrums, yelling, hitting, running in the halls, and inappropriate language. Mr. Juarez is looking for a system to support him and his students. He knows it should not be like this, and he wants to make a change.

Like Mr. Juarez, you may be experiencing challenging behaviors in your classroom, and you may have heard of PBIS. You may have little knowledge of what those four letters mean, but you have likely heard that PBIS may make a difference in your classroom. In fact, I would venture to guess that you would not have chosen this book if you had not at least heard the term PBIS before now. If you selected this book because you believe that PBIS will help you manage behavior challenges in your classroom, you are correct. If you chose this book because you want to implement a system that will benefit the children in your classroom for their entire lives, you are making a good choice. When implemented as designed, PBIS will transform your classroom and your school. I know that probably sounds too good to be true, but stick with me. While PBIS is not a magic potion, it *will* change your classroom. This book will give you everything you need to know to put the PBIS framework to good use in your classroom.

AN EXPLANATION OF THE ACRONYM

Before we talk about how to develop a PBIS system in your classroom, I want to help you better understand the acronym letter by letter: **P**ositive **B**ehavior **I**nterventions and **S**upports. The word **Positive** refers to the fact that we are approaching classroom management from a constructive perspective of teaching and guiding children's behavior instead of punishing. **Behavior** refers to the actions we want children to do in order to be successful both in our classrooms and in the community. Finally, the terms **Interventions** and **Supports** reference the evidence-based practices we use in all three tiers of this framework. In real terms, using PBIS means that we want to create a classroom management system that encourages appropriate child behavior and discourages unwanted behaviors. It also means that we will help young children meet our expectations by using evidence-based strategies—everything we are doing is supported by research.

Right now, I am sure that you are wondering if there is any easy way to do this (and, if not, maybe you can just keep doing what you have always done). Here is the deal: PBIS is hard at first, and there is no way to cheat in implementing it. But I guarantee that if you try what I present in this book, your classroom will change for the better. And even more important, the lives of the children in your classroom will be transformed. When we implement PBIS, we are looking to help young children gain the skills they will need to succeed for the long term. We want to teach them behaviors and actions that will lead to positive outcomes in their lives. Essentially, implementing PBIS in our classrooms shows that we care more about children's futures than about making our lives easy today. Taking the time to use PBIS supports your students and makes an investment in their futures.

PBIS IN A NUTSHELL (WELL, REALLY A TRIANGLE)

Okay, now for the fun part—I get to introduce you to PBIS. "Hi PBIS, this is my friend, Fabulous Teacher. Fabulous Teacher, this is my friend PBIS." All joking aside, I really do think of PBIS as a friend; this framework for teaching success has made my life easier and supported me when I did not know how to help a young child. I sincerely hope that you come to think of PBIS as your teaching friend too.

PBIS has three tiers, levels of support that are designed to meet the needs of young children. The first level, called Tier 1, includes universal supports that are provided to all children in the classroom. Every child, regardless of behavior challenges, receives the supports provided in Tier 1. When Tier 1 is implemented well, it will meet the needs of about 80 to 85 percent of the children in your classroom (Horner and Sugai 2015). The next level of supports is referred to as Tier 2. At this level, evidence-based interventions are provided to small groups of children who need additional support to be successful. About 10 to 15 percent of children will require both Tier 1 and Tier 2 supports (Horner and Sugai 2015). At the top of the pyramid, you will find Tier 3. At this level, we provide the individualized interventions for the 3 percent of young children who have the most challenging behaviors. It is important to note that children receiving Tier 3 interventions still receive both Tiers 1 and 2 supports as well. The figure below provides a simple visual for understanding how the three tiers of PBIS work together to support young children and their teachers. As you proceed through this book, you will likely realize that you are already implementing many of the best practices in the PBIS model, especially those in Tier 1. PBIS uses best practices in early childhood education to increase prosocial behavior and decrease inappropriate behaviors.

Tier 3
Individualized
Interventions

Tier 2
Small-Group Interventions

Tier 1
Universal Prevention Strategies

THE PROOF IS IN THE PUDDING

I bet you are thinking that everything I am saying about PBIS is just too good to be true. You probably think there is no way that PBIS is as magical as I claim it is. Well, the proof is in the pudding, or in the research anyway. There is significant research to support the effectiveness of PBIS at all grade levels, but for our purposes we need only to talk about preschool and kindergarten. Here I provide a brief synopsis of a few of the studies that have proven that using PBIS in early childhood classrooms makes a difference for young children. I want you to hear about real schools that have found success with PBIS.

One study looked at the use of PBIS in ten Head Start classrooms. All of the classrooms in the study implemented both Tiers 1 and 2, and a few of the classrooms also implemented Tier 3. After using PBIS for one school year, the teachers reported that children in these programs had improved social skills and reduced instances of challenging behaviors. In addition, each classroom in the study had a higher score on the Classrom Assessment Scoring System (CLASS) classroom organization domain, an assessment that measures class routines, procedures, and instructional practices. The authors of this study concluded that PBIS leads to improvements for both the classroom as a whole and for individual students (Stanton-Chapman et al. 2016).

Similar results were noted when PBIS was implemented in three rural preschool classrooms. The researchers supported teachers in three years of PBIS implementation. At the end of the period, results of the CLASS assessment showed gains in classroom organization and social skills instruction (Steed et al. 2013).

A third study examined the impact of PBIS for on-task behavior in four preschool classrooms. The teachers used just Tier 1 interventions for the entire class. These interventions include initial instruction on behavioral expectations, pre-correction, praise, and group rewards. After using Tier 1 for one year, the on-task behavior in the classrooms increased by more than 17 percent. In addition, almost 95 percent of the preschool children reported enjoying the activities related to PBIS and particularly mentioned that they enjoyed getting rewards for making the right choice (Jolstead et al. 2017).

PBIS has not only proven to be effective for early childhood classrooms in the United States; international preschools have also implemented this framework and had fantastic results. Szu-Yin Chu (2015) reports that PBIS was used in a Taiwanese preschool and that parents were partners in the implementation. Both off-task behavior and noncompliant behaviors were reduced, and the reduction in challenging behaviors was sustained over time.

As the studies listed indicate, PBIS helps children. At the beginning of this chapter, you read about Mr. Juarez. I suspect that if he began this PBIS process with you, he would experience the results he is seeking. PBIS not only improves behavior but also improves children's social skills. Plus, children report that it is fun!

LET'S GET THIS PARTY STARTED

Now that you know the research supporting the use of PBIS, I hope that you are even more excited about this book and starting this journey with me. Personally, I am pretty thrilled about this (I *might* be dancing with excitement right now). Like any good teacher does, we start our new initiative with a plan of attack. We must brainstorm, research, and develop a specific plan for success before we even think about actually implementing PBIS. The first step is to consider your own classroom and the challenges that exist, to help you recognize how PBIS might fit in. To do this, I have developed a list of twelve questions. I recommend that you take the time to really think about each question and provide a thorough and honest response. Spending a week or two to answer these questions will help things move more smoothly later in this process. I have outlined the questions, which appear on the form in appendix A, and provided an explanation of what to consider as you answer each one.

Question 1: Why do I want to implement PBIS?

We should always think about our "why" when making decisions. So the first (and most important) question to ask yourself is why you are considering PBIS at all. Why do you want to undertake a huge initiative? Are you only doing it because your boss says you have to? (If this is your answer, I suggest that you take time to consider why your boss might be asking you to try this and find motivation to give it a try.) Are you, like Mr. Juarez, feeling desperate because the behavior challenges in your classroom are so bad that you have no idea what to do? Do you feel that things in your classroom are going well but could be just a little better? Do you want a new challenge? Were you impressed by the cover of this book and thought, "Hey, why not?" Take time to really think about the answer to this question. Your answer will guide the entire process of PBIS implementation, and your answer will look different from the answers of others.

Question 2: What challenging behaviors exist in my classroom?

Young children exhibit a wide range of behaviors that may be considered challenging. To effectively implement PBIS in your classroom, you must consider what specific behavior challenges exist in your classroom. Are the children wiggly? Are they loud or do they yell a lot? Do they hit, kick, or bite? Do they forget to clean up their mess after snacktime or neglect to wash their hands after using the toilet? Are your instructions to children often met with argument? List as many challenging behaviors as you can think of that are regular occurrences or sources of concern.

I don't know about you, but for me, days of teaching can get so busy that I don't remember everything that happened at the end of the day. After a long day, I am hard-pressed to make a list of behaviors or other events that occurred. To get a clear picture of the behaviors in your classroom, I recommend soliciting help and taking a little data. Did you just panic a little bit when you read the word *data*? Don't worry—appendix B provides a reproducible data collection chart. Make a few copies, put them on a clipboard, grab a pen, and let's get started. If there are multiple adults in the classroom, each of you should do this. Two (or more) heads are better than one since it's likely one person will miss some behaviors. The data collection chart in appendix B is very simple, but right now simple is all you need. In the first column, write the time of day. You don't need to be completely accurate—you can write the approximate time of day or the activity that is going on. For example, you might write "9:00" or "circle time." The second column asks for the name of the child doing the behavior. To make it simpler, I recommend just putting the first letter of the child's name here (or if two children have the same first letter, then put the child's initials). The final column asks you to list the behavior. Again, keep it simple; list just one word if possible. You might write, "yell" or "bit."

If you can, collect this data for an entire week. I know that might feel like a lot, especially when you are anxious to get started with addressing challenging behaviors in your classroom, but taking this time now will lead to better results later. Having more initial (also called *baseline*) data to consider will lead to a stronger PBIS system and let you make plans that are specific to your needs and the needs of the children in your classroom. Better planning on the front end leads to better results overall.

After a week of data collection, it is time to analyze that data. Brew yourself a cup of coffee, grab your favorite pen and a highlighter, and let's tackle this data! On a new sheet of paper, make a list of the behaviors included on your data collection charts. Make a tally mark for each time the behavior is noted. Once you are done, take your highlighter and highlight the three or four behaviors that are listed most frequently. These are the most challenging behaviors in your classroom. The figure below provides an example of how this will look.

• Yelling	ЖЖЖЖЖЖ IIII
• Wiggling	ЖЖ IIII
• Running around classroom	Ж III
• Biting	II
• Saying "no" to teacher directions	ЖЖЖ II
• Stealing toys	ЖЖЖЖЖ I
• Hitting	Ж II
• Throwing trash from snack onto floor	III
• Not washing hands after using toilet	ЖЖЖЖЖЖЖЖ IIII
• Kicking	IIII
• Spitting at others	I

In the chart, you can easily see that yelling, stealing toys, and not washing hands are the most problematic behaviors in this fictional classroom. The next step is figuring out when and where those behaviors are happening. Follow the same procedure to determine the two or three places where behaviors tend to occur (see appendix B). You do not need to list the specific behaviors, but just note that there was a challenging behavior during that time period.

An example is included below. You can see that for this example, center time, snacktime, and outdoor free play are the most problematic activities each day. Having a higher number of behavior challenges during unstructured times is common. You may find that your results are similar, with the highest numbers of behavior incidents happening during centers, snack/lunch, or playtime. The exercise is valuable, however, because it may help you uncover learning times that are also unexpectedly problematic.

Arrival/table activities	‖‖ ‖‖
Morning circle time	‖
Literacy learning time	‖‖
Morning centers time	‖‖ ‖‖ ‖‖ ‖‖
Snacktime	‖‖ ‖‖
Morning outdoor free play	‖‖ ‖‖ ‖‖ ‖‖ ‖
Math learning time	‖
Lunch	‖‖ ‖
Rest time/teacher lunch break	‖
Afternoon centers time	‖‖ ‖‖ ‖‖ ‖
Afternoon outdoor free play	‖‖ ‖‖ ‖‖ ‖‖ ‖‖
Afternoon circle time	‖‖
Packing up/going home	‖

Question 3: Are these behaviors a problem for all students or just a few?

You have now determined which behaviors occur most frequently, as well as when those behaviors occur. In addition, you have an understanding of all other behaviors that, while less frequent, still cause a problem. The third piece of data that we need to look at is the "who" of the behaviors. Create another chart, this time with children's names or initials. For one or two days, make a quick tally mark each time a particular child engages in an inappropriate behavior. You do not need to list the behaviors, but you can if you would like. At the end of your one- or two-day data collection period, look at the chart. Are all children equally represented, or are there a few children with most of the tally marks? Based on your knowledge so far this school year, is this chart an accurate representation of behaviors in your classroom? If you are not sure or if you do not believe the chart is accurate, take data for a couple more days. If you do believe it is accurate, move on to question 4.

In my sample chart, you can see that just a few children seem to be involved in the majority of challenging behaviors in the classroom. Amber, Jin, and Raúl each had more than 15 tally marks in one day. The rest of the children had five or fewer tally marks. This simple chart shows me that no child is perfect (really, who is?), but most of my current behavior management is likely focused on three of the ten children.

Amber	||||| ||||| ||||| ||||
Asa		
Clementine	||||
Colby	||
Jin	||||| ||||| ||||| ||||| ||||| ||||| ||||
Kamal		
Kayden	|||
Raúl	||||| ||||| |||||	
Su		
Zayden	||

Question 4: Who are the most challenging students in my classroom?

Looking at the example, you can see that one child really stands out: Jin, with thirty-four tally marks. The second most come from Amber, with eighteen tally marks, and then Raúl, with sixteen. This information will become very important later, so hold on to it. I will also caution you to be careful with this knowledge. At this point, it can be very easy to see Jin as a "problem" since the majority of the behavior issues in your classroom are from him. However, please remember that Jin is a small child. He is not a "problem"; he is just a child who needs your support. Your decision to try PBIS in your classroom is one way that you can (and will) help and support Jin. Personally, I want to thank you for caring enough about Jin to try out PBIS. You are awesome, and Jin is lucky to be in your class.

I also want to remind you that this data is just a small snapshot of what is going on in your classroom. When you look at all of the tally marks, you may feel overwhelmed or may begin to think that your class is horribly behaved. Don't believe any of that nonsense! You are lucky to be the teacher for a fabulous classroom full of young learners, and you get the special privilege of guiding them in their future growth and development, including learning appropriate social behaviors. Frankly, you have the best job in the world.

Question 5: Which adults work in my classroom?

As you begin to make plans for implementing PBIS in your classroom, you need to consider the resources you have available. One of the most valuable resources in any classroom is people. Make a list of the adults who work in your room and include in your list how much time they spend with you. Be sure to include parent volunteers, both those who help in your classroom and those who are willing to spend time at home to create learning materials for you. Each of the people on your list can (and should) be a part of your support system and should be involved in the PBIS planning process. After making this list, you may find that you have a lot of adults helping you, or, conversely, that you have very little adult support in your classroom. Keep in mind that a fantastic PBIS program can be implemented by just one person or by a group of people, so regardless of the answer to this question, you can do this!

Question 6: What specific routines must I follow?

The next topic I want you to consider is the structure of your day. What must be included in your day? Are there certain times that you must complete certain activities (for example, you may have an assigned playground time from 10:00 to 11:00 every morning). How much flexibility do you have with routines and the timing of activities? A sample answer to this question is provided. As you can see, this teacher has a lot of flexibility, but there are a few activities (specifically outdoor time and the teacher's lunch break) that cannot be moved to a different time of day. Looking at this chart will help him see that he has the option to move morning centers time before circle time, if that would work better. Or, he can choose to do literacy learning time just before lunch and move math learning time earlier in the morning. Having knowledge about your daily routine will help as you work through chapter 6 and specifically teach the classroom routine and adjust it as necessary to meet the needs of your classroom.

Arrival/table activities	8:30–8:45
Morning circle time	Timing is flexible.
Literacy learning time	Timing is flexible.
Morning centers time	Timing is flexible.
Snacktime	Timing is flexible but needs to be midmorning.
Morning outdoor free play	10:00–11:00
Math learning time	Timing is flexible.
Lunch	Timing is flexible but needs to be about noon and must be completed and cleaned up before 12:50 to prepare for rest time.
Rest time/teacher lunch break	1:00–2:00
Afternoon centers time	Timing is flexible.
Afternoon outdoor free play	2:00–2:30
Afternoon circle time	3:00–3:20
Packing up/going home	3:20–3:30

Question 7: What is the classroom layout, and do I have the freedom to rearrange it?

In some cases, the layout of a classroom can affect children's behavior. A busy classroom layout can make it difficult for a teacher to see all of the children and stop challenging behaviors before they start or address challenging behaviors quickly. A preferred center located right next to the circle time carpet may distract children who would prefer to play in the center instead of participating in circle time.

Create a simple drawing of the classroom layout. In addition, consider how much control you have over the arrangement of the classroom. If you share the room with another teacher, or furniture is permanently attached to the wall or floor, you may not be able to rearrange much. It may be helpful to color-code your drawing to indicate furniture that is permanently attached and furniture that can be moved.

Question 8: What systems do I use to communicate with stakeholders about my classroom?

Communication with all stakeholders (including parents, other teachers, and classroom assistants) is an important part of implementing any new concept in the classroom. PBIS is no different. If you want to ensure quality outcomes for your efforts, you need to have a way to communicate with other adults. In fact, you will likely be more effective if you use a variety of communication methods to ensure your message is received. These could include face-to-face conversations, phone calls, text messages, smartphone apps, emails, handwritten notes, a print newsletter, or a classroom blog. List the ways that you communicate with stakeholders, and be specific about which methods you use to communicate with different groups of people. Then consider how effective those communication systems are for meeting your current needs. Is there a method of communication that seems to be preferred or one that rarely gets a response? What methods of communication do your stakeholders seem to prefer, and do those methods align with how you are doing most of your communication?

Question 9: What are the learning goals that my students must achieve?

Ultimately, the goal in any classroom is student learning. In a preschool classroom, this includes academic, social, and behavioral learning. Think about the big-picture learning goals that need to be accomplished between now and the end of the school year, and make a short list. As you begin PBIS implementation (and evaluate its effectiveness later on), this list will help you determine how well your intervention is working. Ultimately, even if student behavior is perfect, if you have not met these learning goals, you have not achieved the expectations for this school year. Remember that one of our goals with PBIS is to increase children's learning and set them up for long-term success.

Question 10: What resources do I have available to support me in implementing PBIS?

As you begin to think about planning your PBIS implementation, you should make a list of resources that will be available to support you. This list should include people, materials, financial support, and time. Be sure to include the adults that you listed as the answer to question 5. You may find it helpful to create a table and list the resources available in each of the four categories. Please remember that money and resources are not necessary for excellent instruction; you can create a fabulous PBIS program even if your list of resources is minimal. An example list of resources is provided below. You will notice that this teacher does not have a lot of resources listed but that she is willing to think outside of the box to acquire what she needs to support student learning. Please note that you may not need to use all of the resources you have available to you (especially your spouse's time or the funding of local businesses), but I recommend listing any resource you can access, just in case.

PEOPLE	MATERIALS	FINANCIAL SUPPORT	TIME
• Classroom assistant (in classroom during my lunch break) • School floater (sometimes available to assist with special projects) • Preschool director • Parents of the children in my classroom (most cannot help in the classroom other than parties, but maybe they can do projects at home) • My spouse (may be willing to help create materials at home)	• Books on social skills/behavior • Public library books for teaching concepts • Puppets • Art supplies • Stickers for prizes • Classroom treasure box	• $50 annual supplies budget • Parents may be willing to donate money or materials • I could ask local businesses for donations, if needed	• One hour planning time each week

Question 11: What challenges do I foresee in PBIS implementation?

Like any new idea, PBIS will come with challenges. You can better address those challenges if you create a plan before they arise. Challenges may be large or small, but they all must be addressed to be best set up for success. Challenges that might occur include other adults undermining the work you are doing, students not consistently showing up for school, not having enough time to complete everything, your own absences (family situations, illness, and so on), feeling overwhelmed by the extra work, and understanding how to use the data to enhance children's behavior and learning.

Question 12: What are my fears about attempting PBIS?

I don't know about you, but I have a lot of fears (hello, mice and heights). I also get very nervous when I try something new for my students. I am terrified that it won't work (or sometimes, I am scared that it will work too well!). Being scared or nervous is completely normal, but you can better prepare to manage your fears if you address them early. Knowing your fears can help you face them head on. Make a list of the things that scare you about PBIS. Common fears might be that it will take too much time, that behavior challenges will increase instead of decreasing, or that other adults in the classroom will not follow the plan and cancel out the hard work a teacher is doing.

Appendix A provides a form with these twelve questions in a format you can print and complete. I recommend that you and all other adults working in your classroom complete this form at this time. Remember that you will likely spend a week or two completing it. You don't want to rush this step, so take your time and do a thorough job.

MOVING FORWARD

Now that you have begun to think about PBIS implementation and have completed the twelve-question document, it is time to share with others that you are planning changes in your classroom. You need to ensure that all stakeholders (this includes other adults working in your classroom, school administrators, parents, and potentially school board members) understand what you are doing. When they understand PBIS, they will be better able to assist you in making it a reality. Appendix C provides a short synopsis of PBIS that you can provide to classroom assistants and other adults working in your classroom. I would urge them to consider reading this book as well, but appendix C will give them a strong starting point for understanding what you want to accomplish in your classroom. In appendix D, you will find a sample letter that you can send to parents to introduce the idea of PBIS. Use the letter as written or modify it to meet the needs of the families you serve.

Once you have shared the excitement of PBIS with everyone around you, it is time to move forward with this thrilling journey. This will be one wild roller coaster ride, but it is going to be awesome! Take a deep breath, grab some more coffee and a snack, and meet me in chapter 3.

CHAPTER 3

PBIS Practices at All Levels

Ms. Raines has been teaching in the same classroom in the same small community for thirty-five years. Each year lately, the class closely resembles the class composition from the year before, with an almost equal mix of children from Caucasian, African American, and Hispanic backgrounds. Ms. Raines has used the same holiday celebrations every year. This year, though, things have changed. One of the families in her class has adopted a child from Uganda, and they are asking her to incorporate some of his cultural traditions into her celebrations. Ms. Raines thinks this sounds like a lovely idea, but she is just not sure how to do that.

Like Ms. Raines, you likely have a diverse classroom of children. They come from a variety of backgrounds. The children have different family structures, religions, cultures, attitudes, beliefs, and personal experiences. The new student in Ms. Raines's classroom has likely had life experiences that are different from his classmates. As you prepare to teach the children in your classroom and implement PBIS, it is critical that you use several best practices, including showing respect for each child, showing respect for the cultures represented in your classroom, using evidence-based practices and action-research to guide the decisions you make about instruction and behavior management.

RESPECT FOR THE CHILD

Knowing that each child who enters our classroom is a unique individual helps us ensure that we treat them as such. As you use PBIS in your classroom, it is vital that every decision you make shows that you respect young children. When a child in our classroom consistently struggles to meet our behavioral expectations (or, worse yet, we have an entire class like that), it is easy to begin thinking of the child as a problem. Without meaning to, we may quickly find ourselves making statements (either as thoughts in our heads or verbally to other adults or even to the children) like "Billy is such a problem" or "Guadalupe is so naughty!" When we make comments such as these, we lose sight of the child as a person and instead begin focusing on his or her faults. Can you imagine what it must be like for people to see only your faults and ignore all of the good in you? (I am personally thankful that people are able to see beyond my poor housekeeping skills and notice my talents!) I challenge you to focus on the good in all of the children in your classroom. I think it helps to view challenging behavior as a sign that the child needs help with something. So instead of thinking about how much harder my job becomes when children "don't behave," I tell myself that bad behaviors are one way that young children tell me they need help. Then, I get to crack the code of how I can help them—I get to be a little bit like Nancy Drew and save the day by solving mysteries that help children. (Cool, huh?)

One method I recommend that will help you focus more on children as unique people and less on the challenges they present in the classroom is to create a document about the children. Appendix E provides a printable form for thinking about the children in your classroom. The form allows for you to include the information for only four children, so you will likely need to print a few copies to take notes about all of the children you teach. I highly recommend that every adult who works in the classroom complete these forms, either individually or as a group. By sharing each of your experiences with the children and your knowledge of them, you will get a better picture of each child.

Appendix F asks you to think about each child and the characteristics that define them. Think about what makes Suzie different from Johnny (beyond just their genders). Who are these children as individuals? What do you need to know to best support them in growing, while still allowing them to be themselves? Specifically, you should provide information about each child in the five areas of family, personality and interests, needs, beliefs, and any other important information. As you complete this form, I recommend that you take time to consider your own personal culture and bias, as well as the impact your own experiences have on your expectations of children (see pages 26–28 for more on this). When completing appendixes E and F, you will need to be careful not to make judgments about each child and their family but instead just to report the facts. You may find that you can get answers to many of the questions through a questionnaire sent home to parents, but be aware that not every parent will complete those forms. Be prepared to learn this information in other ways too.

1. Family Structure

Include notes about the structure of the child's family and any important information about the family. Who lives with the child? Who is/are the primary caregiver(s) for the child? Does the child live in more than one house? Are there siblings in the home? What about pets? How long has the child lived with the current family structure? How long has the family lived at that current address? What is their relationship with their extended family? In addition, you should include information about any adverse childhood experiences (ACEs) of which you are aware; these might include witnessing, or being the victim of, abuse or violence, homelessness, poverty, a family member dying by suicide, or a parent in prison. For more information about ACEs and the impact they have on young children, I suggest looking at the fact sheet on the Centers for Disease Control (CDC) website (www.cdc.gov/violenceprevention /aces/fastfact.html).

2. Personality and Interests

Make notes about the child as an individual. Is she quiet with a tendency to sit in the corner and observe classmates? Is he loud and always in motion? Does she seem to prefer playing with others? Does he like to play alone? To what toys and activities does she gravitate? Does he always head to the block center the moment you announce centers time? Does she spend hours looking at books in the classroom library? Does he tell you about the latest episode of *Paw Patrol* the moment he arrives at school every morning? Does she often tell you that she is hoping to go to the park when her dad picks her up after school? As you get to know the children in your classroom better, this column may change or expand, so I recommend taking notes in pencil. Because this column can (and likely should) be very long, I also recommend that you include a few key words that describe each child. To help you have both a thorough description of each child as well as this quick classroom snapshot, appendix F provides a form that you can complete for each child; I recommend keeping the completed appendix F forms in each child's individual file. Additionally, your knowledge and understanding of each child will grow significantly if you ask the children to help you complete the forms about themselves. I once taught a little girl who always wore dresses but refused to wear tights, leggings, or pants under her dress, even when it was cold outside. Her mom did the same thing, so I assumed that she was trying to be like her mommy. One day I simply asked her. Our conversation is described below.

> ME: Hey, Sally, I love that beautiful dress you are wearing today. The pretty pink flowers make you look like a princess! I have a silly question, though. Don't your legs get really cold when we go to the playground? I have some extra tights you can wear while we go outside; would you like to borrow them?
>
> SALLY: No! I don't like tights! They feel itchy on my legs!
>
> ME: Oh, I understand. Well, what about these leggings or jeans that I have? Would you like to wear one of these? These leggings have pretty pink flowers, just like your dress.
>
> SALLY: No! Everything feels itchy on my legs! I don't like it! I like being cold more than I like being itchy!

Up until this conversation, I had mistakenly assumed that Sally had bare legs as a style preference (and, isn't it amazing how style conscious young children can be?). But after talking to Sally, I learned how very wrong I was. She was choosing to be cold due to a sensory concern, not for style. Remember that our assumptions can be wrong, so it is always best practice to gain clarification from a child.

If I was to complete the assessment from appendix F for my son, Abraham (age five), I would include the following information: He likes blue. His favorite books are the Llama Llama series by Anna Dewdney (and this mama's heart melts every time he calls me Mama Llama). He loves to play Paw Patrol Memory, and his favorite toys are trucks. He would spend all day watching *Paw Patrol* or *Octonauts* and eating cereal if I let him. He is an observer and prefers to watch other children first before playing with them, but once he is comfortable with another child, he is a loyal friend and will do anything for friends. He is seemingly fearless and is constantly climbing on something unsafe. He loves to listen to stories, build with Lego bricks, and play on the slide. He adores being with his sisters, going to the zoo, and helping Daddy build things in the shed. He does not like being forced to sit at the table for mealtimes nor getting dressed. After reading that, I suspect that you now have a pretty solid picture of Abraham. This picture is the goal of appendix F. When completed, this form should provide all adults with a quick understanding of the child.

3. Needs

Include physical and emotional needs in this column. Does he take medicines? Does she need a nap to function well? Does he need a few minutes of one-on-one time with the teacher first thing every morning? Does she need to be left alone when she gets upset? Does he need to be alerted before arriving at school if something will be unusual, such as the teacher being absent or a special visitor coming? Does she need the opportunity to wiggle in her chair? List any and all needs you can think of that are specific to the child in this column. You do not need to include the basic needs of all children, such as food, rest, playtime, and attention, unless the child needs more of one of these things than most other children.

4. Beliefs

Take notes on the family's beliefs and cultural background. Does the family practice a certain faith? Has the family recently moved from another country or another part of the United States (as someone who loved living in Texas for eight years, for example, I can attest that the state has a culture all of its own!). The new student in Ms. Raines's class will probably celebrate different holidays, or the same holidays in different ways, than his classmates. Is the family vegetarian or vegan? What are the family's beliefs about the role of a teacher in caring for and educating children? As you complete this column, think about the effect family beliefs may have on the child and how you can incorporate those beliefs into your classroom.

5. Other Important Information

This column allows you to take note of anything else that might be relevant or important about the child or the family. Which parent should you call first in the event of an emergency? Does Dad work across the street? Is the child a neighbor or sibling of another child in the school? Does he have any allergies? Is she scared of the fire alarm?

By taking the time to complete appendix F, you are setting yourself up to successfully showing respect for each child as a unique individual. Earlier I mentioned my son Abraham. On page 26, you will find a completed Classroom Snapshot Form for Abraham to help you better understand how to complete this. You will notice that I have included single words from appendix F to complete the personality/interests section.

NAME OF CHILD	FAMILY STRUCTURE	PERSONALITY AND INTERESTS	NEEDS	BELIEFS (CULTURE/ RELIGION)	OTHER IMPORTANT INFORMATION
Abraham	Lives with Dad, Mom, 3 sisters (ages 12, 10, and 6), and 2 dogs	Observer Climber Blue *Llama Llama* *Paw Patrol* *Octonauts* Trucks Lego	1:1 attention several times during the day Ability to make choices about activities	Protestant	New to school this year Mom is best person to contact, via phone, text, or email

RESPECT FOR CHILDREN'S CULTURE

Just as it is important that we show deep respect for children, it is equally critical to be respectful of all children's cultures and beliefs. It can be easy to design expectations that align with what we personally believe, but we need to ensure that our PBIS system also aligns with the cultures represented in our classroom. For example, in some cultures, it is considered an insult to make the thumbs-up sign. Because this differs from traditional American cultural norms, children may be regarded as other or misinterpreted for refusing to use this sign in the classroom. To ensure that you are not creating classroom expectations that will set children up for failure because they differ so drastically from cultural norms, I recommend the following practices.

1. Talk to parents/caregivers about cultural norms. In most cases, the parents or caregivers of young children are more than happy to talk to you about their family's beliefs and traditions. But they are unlikely to do so unless you ask. So, ask! Ask general questions. Ask specific questions. Ask them what they think you should know.

2. Learn about the culture. As teachers, we love learning, and we especially love learning new things that will help us to better teach young children. Use your own love of learning to research the cultures represented in

your classroom. Go to the public library to check out books. Take a few minutes during your lunch break to look up information and teaching ideas online. Seek out community members and friends with a similar cultural background as the child; ask for their advice. Ask your colleagues, especially those who have worked with the child or family before, for ideas and advice.

3. Always assume the best intentions of children. If children consistently do not comply with your expectations, dig a little further into what is happening before assuming the child is simply being noncompliant. Early in my career, I worked with a teacher who got very upset when children would not look her in the eye while she was talking to them or when they were talking to her; she believed that not making eye contact indicated that they were not listening to her or that they were lying to her. She frequently punished a little girl for always looking down when she spoke, as the teacher believed that the child was telling lies. The teacher began telling others in the school that "Rosie is such a liar. I never know when she is being truthful. I hope you never have to deal with her!" As I mentioned earlier, many cultures believe that eye contact is disrespectful. That was the case for Rosie; she was not lying but was in fact showing her respect for the teacher. Simply because of the mismatch between the teacher's expectations and Rosie's cultural expectations, Rosie was labeled a troublemaker.

In addition to ensuring that your classroom expectations are respectful of students' cultures and backgrounds, you can show respect through several other practices, as outlined here.

1. Invite parents to visit the classroom to share about their culture. They can give a short presentation, tell a story, read a book, or simply answer children's questions. I highly recommend that they include their own child in this process, as it will help the child better understand himself and will help classmates understand the family's background.

2. Include books in the classroom library that reflect the cultures represented in the classroom as well as a variety of other cultures and backgrounds.

3. Celebrate holidays from each culture. This can sometimes be overwhelming, and you might end up feeling like you are constantly having a party.

But remember that young children learn from experiences, and celebrations can be a fun way to teach them about cultures other than their own as well as about showing respect to others. In addition, hosting holiday celebrations can be an excellent opportunity to include parents and other caregivers in the classroom. Ask them if they are willing to help plan the celebration.

The table includes a short list of books that I recommend including in your classroom library to help create an appreciation for diversity; please note that this list is not exhaustive, and books alone will not create an accepting atmosphere in your classroom. While it is critical that you include children's cultures and backgrounds in your classroom, I will caution you to remember that every culture has subcultures, and every family has its own culture. Not every child from the same culture will have the same background.

BOOK	AUTHOR
Global Babies	The Global Fund for Children
Global Baby Boys	Maya Ajmera
Global Baby Girls	The Global Fund for Children
Families	Star Bright Books
Whoever You Are	Mem Fox
Boozhoo: Come Play with Us	Fond du Lac Head Start
A Piece of Home	Jeri Watts
Ten Little Fingers and Ten Little Toes	Mem Fox
Last Stop on Market Street	Matt de la Peña
I Love My Hair!	Natasha Anastasia Tarpley
I Am Enough	Grace Byers
Skin Like Mine	LaTashia M. Perry

EVIDENCE-BASED PRACTICES

Like you, I want to ensure that I am spending my time and energy in the most efficient manner for the benefit of children and families. I want to use teaching practices that I know work instead of wasting time doing things that are ineffective. For example, when I teach a child to read, I use a phonics-based curriculum because the use of phonics is proven to be effective. One way to increase the likelihood of getting the most payoff for my efforts in the classroom is the use of evidence-based practices. According to the Every Student Succeeds Act (which as of 2020 is the foremost education law in the United States), evidence-based practices are teaching practices that are supported by research. Essentially, it means that there is solid evidence that tells you these teaching practices work. Locating evidence-based practices can be challenging, and I have provided a table of reliable websites for locating these ideas. As you prepare to implement PBIS in your classroom, it is critical that you are using evidence-based practices in all three tiers. The strategies and interventions outlined in this book all meet the standards of evidence-based practice.

RESOURCE	WEBSITE
What Works Clearinghouse	https://ies.ed.gov/ncee/wwc
Education Resources Information Center (ERIC)	https://eric.ed.gov
Center on the Social and Emotional Foundations for Early Learning	http://csefel.vanderbilt.edu
National Center for Pyramid Model Innovations	http://challengingbehavior.cbcs.usf.edu
Early Childhood Technical Assistance Center	http://ectacenter.org

ACTION-RESEARCH IN YOUR CLASSROOM

As you begin to implement evidence-based practices, you will need to evaluate their effectiveness in your classroom. Remember that even the best interventions may not work for every student or in every classroom every single day. To determine if the teaching practice is right for your classroom, you will need to conduct action-research and take data. Action-research is simply using data to make informed decisions about teaching and learning in your classroom. And when you use it, you can tell all of your friends and family that you are a researcher.

I *love* data. In fact, that is likely a huge understatement. Just thinking about data makes me want to break out into a song and dance. In the classroom, I love (love, love, love, love) data because it tells me whether my efforts are having the intended outcome. I really hate to waste time, so I want to know if the work I am doing is making a difference for children and their families. If the initiatives I begin are not changing children's behaviors, then I need to make a change in how I am implementing PBIS. This is where classroom data comes in—I need to take data to better understand the results of my work and then use that data to make adjustments to my instruction and interventions.

As you worked through the questions in chapter 2, you completed preliminary data collection in appendix B. Most data collection will be as simple as that form (and, in fact, I recommend you continue using that same form while you implement Tier 1 and on occasion throughout the school year). Taking notes about behaviors you observe can be a simple but effective form of data collection. As we get to more challenging student behaviors, beginning in chapter 8, we will talk more specifically about how to collect data that will be used to support specific students. For now, I just want you to think about the need for, and value in, data collection. And, maybe, just maybe, you can do a little data song and dance too (and if you do, please send me a video—I love data dances)!

MOVING FORWARD

You have now made it one-fourth of the way through this book. How are you feeling? Are you as excited as I am about the next steps of PBIS implementation? Are you feeling a little nervous? (Don't worry—you are doing great!) As you prepare to move to chapter 4, let's quickly recap chapter 3: at all levels of PBIS and in all classroom instruction, you should ensure that you are demonstrating respect for all students, showing respect for the cultures represented in your classroom, using evidence-based practices, and conducting action-research to evaluate whether your instruction is working. Next we will begin to explore creating a foundation for student success in Tier 1 by collaborating with families.

CHAPTER 4

Tier 1 Intervention: Collaboration with Families

Mr. Sanders teaches in a Head Start program. He knows that working with parents and other caregivers has long-term positive effects for young children, so he is intentional about building relationships with caregivers and providing ways for parents/guardians to become active participants in their children's learning and development. He begins each school year by visiting families at home and has made a habit of calling parents on a weekly basis. He welcomes families into his classroom for special events but also encourages them to visit whenever they would like. In his weekly newsletter, he reminds parents that they are welcome to stick around after dropping off their children or come early at pickup time. Mr. Sanders has noticed that when he approaches parents about challenging behaviors, they seem receptive to what he has to say and are often willing to partner with him in addressing the challenges.

As Mr. Sanders knows, one critical aspect of teaching children of all ages, but especially young children, is collaborating with families. Regardless of how much time children spend in the school setting, their parents are the most important and longest-lasting teachers in their lives. As early childhood teachers, we get the pleasure of teaching children for one or two years, but their parents have the joy and responsibility of teaching them for eighteen years (or more). Success in the early childhood classroom depends on collaboration between teachers and families, and that collaboration is enhanced when teachers intentionally build relationships with families before challenges arise.

In the PBIS model, working as a team helps teachers and families prevent potential challenging behaviors and address them when they do occur. This collaborative relationship between parents and schools is a critical aspect of Tier 1 PBIS, and developing these relationships should be part of your instructional practice even before children enter your classroom.

TEAMWORK MAKES THE DREAM WORK

Research supports the positive impacts that happen when schools and families work together. For addressing challenging behaviors, teaming with families makes a huge difference. A 2017 report funded by the US Department of Education Office for Special Education Programs notes the need to involve families in effective classroom behavior management and cites the research that effective teaming with families leads to fewer challenging behaviors, especially for young children with disabilities (Weist et al. 2017). In addition, home and school collaboration increases desirable prosocial skills, such as sharing, communication, problem-solving, and social interaction. Basically, this super long and dense report says that if you work with parents, your job will be easier and the children in your classroom will be more successful in both the short term and the long term.

HOME VISITS

Before the school year begins, I recommend visiting children and families at home. Schedule a time to visit, meet the family, see the child's favorite toys, and socialize with their pets. The child will likely feel more comfortable in their own home and may feel less nervous about meeting you. Keep in mind, though, that parents are likely to feel nervous about having you in their home. You will need to assure them that you are not there to judge them but instead to create a partnership in order to support their child. I also suggest recommending an alternative place to meet if they would prefer not to host you in their home or if you would prefer not to visit homes. Possible meeting places might include a local park, restaurant, or public library. Just be sure that the meeting place is familiar to (and preferred by) the child. When children enter your classroom mid–school year, or if you work in a school that has rolling admission and the class composition changes throughout the year, I suggest using these same strategies to welcome each new child and family into your classroom.

If home visits are not an option for you, there are other ways to make a connection with children and families before children enter your classroom. Of course there are situations in which students join your your class without warning, and in those situations I recommend using the following suggestions during the child's first week or two in your classroom. Ideas include the following:

1. Call each family to introduce yourself and answer any questions they may have. During the phone call, ask for the opportunity to say hello to the child.

2. Schedule an online video chat with the family using a service such as Zoom or Skype. This will allow you to see one another and will feel more personal than a phone call. In addition, it will likely be less intimidating for many parents than having you in their home.

3. Send a postcard to the child and a letter to the parents. Young children love receiving mail and will be excited to get a note from you. Parents will appreciate having an initial connection with you before meeting you in person. The figure below shows a basic sample letter that you can adapt to send to the parents in your classroom.

Dear Mr. and Mrs. Ruiz,

My name is Mrs. Lohmann, and I have the distinct pleasure of being Raúl's preschool teacher this school year. I have been teaching preschool for five years, and this is my second year at Happy Days Early Learning Center. I absolutely love teaching and cannot wait for this school year to begin.

One of my favorite parts of being a teacher is teaming with parents to meet the needs of children. I am very excited to partner with you to support Raúl's growth and development. To begin our partnership, I would love to schedule a meeting (via phone, web-based, or in person) at your convenience. Please call me at 555-123-4567 or email me at lohmann@preschool.com to schedule a time to meet.

I can't wait to talk to you!

Mrs. Lohmann

COMMUNICATE WITH PARENTS

As the school year progresses, make time to contact parents on a regular basis. Like Mr. Sanders at the beginning of the chapter, make intentional communication with families part of your daily or weekly routine. Call, email, text, speak in person, and send notes home. When communicating with families, I recommend that you document all conversations. This can help you remember what you have discussed as well as provide proof of those conversations in the event of a problem later. One easy way to document these conversations is to keep a family-school communication log for each child in your classroom. These can be paper logs that are kept in a file folder, or you can create a folder for this information on your computer (spreadsheet software such as Microsoft Excel or Google Sheets works well for this purpose). Use a method that works for you—that is what is important. The log should also include the contact information for family members. Be consistent in documenting conversations. You can find a sample completed log below as well as a printable log for your use in appendix G.

Child Name: Suzie

DATE/TIME	METHOD OF COMMUNICATION	TOPIC OF CONVERSATION	FOLLOW-UP ACTIONS/NOTES
August 1	Mailed letter	Introduced myself and requested to schedule meeting	Parent will contact me to schedule meeting
August 8	Home visit	Introduction, answer questions	
August 9	Email	Thank you for letting me visit	Parent should complete "Getting to Know My Child" form—completed and returned on August 19
August 15	Class newsletter	Welcome to class, class procedures	
August 20	Phone call to mom	Thank you for returning the "Getting to Know My Child" form	Mom said that she likes phone calls, but they need to be in the evening so she does not get into trouble for being on the phone at work
August 21	Email	Recap of phone conversation, reiterated that I will make weekly phone call in the evenings	

To ensure that I was communicating with parents on a consistent basis, I used to choose one day per week to call the parents of all of my students. For me, it was every Thursday afternoon so that I could share the big events of the week. In addition, I recommend a handwritten personal note or email as a follow-up. I like to send emails on Friday mornings as a quick follow-up to the Thursday phone calls. Even a very simple and basic email can go a long way in building your relationship with the family. A sample follow-up Friday email is below. As you find new ways to communicate with parents, remember to keep track of your conversations using the form in appendix G.

> Dear Mrs. Ruiz,
>
> Thank you for taking the time to speak with me yesterday afternoon. I really enjoy teaming with you to support Raúl's development. As I mentioned on the phone, Raúl has had a great week, and I have noticed a significant increase in his turn-taking skills this week. Yesterday morning, he played four games of Go Fish and did a fantastic job of waiting his turn! I am so proud of him! As I also noted, he had a few bathroom accidents this week. This is completely normal, and I am not concerned about this. I know that you mentioned that he is having accidents at home as well. Just keep reminding him to use the toilet and use a timer to remind him every twenty to thirty minutes, if necessary. Thanks again for partnering with me in supporting Raúl. I love chatting with you, and I am so happy to see the progress that Raúl is making. Have a fabulous weekend!
>
> Mrs. Lohmann

SEND "HOMEWORK" CALENDARS

While I firmly believe that homework should not be required in the preschool classroom, I also know that many parents of young children want to be more involved in their children's education. Based on my experience, however, many parents are simply unsure of what to do to best support their children and are seeking ideas from experts in the field of education, like yourself. So, I recommend creating optional homework or an optional homework calendar. I do suggest, though, that you are careful to keep it simple and not overwhelming. By supporting parents in becoming more involved in their children's learning, you will enhance your relationship with them. And you are likely to find that once parents start becoming involved in the education process, they want to be more and more involved. A sample homework sheet for celebrating autumn can be found here.

Lohmann's Lions October Homework

Dear Parents,

Welcome to the month of October. Our school year is starting off fabulously, and we are having a great time learning together. This month we will celebrate autumn, and I would love for the children's learning to extend into your homes. Below, please find a list of *optional* activities that you and your child can complete together this month. After completing an activity, your child can put one of the attached stickers on top of it. Please note that all of the listed books are available at the local public library, and I also have an extra copy of each book that you can check out from me. I would love to see photos and hear stories about your experiences this month, so please send them my way via email (lohmann@preschool.com) or tell me a story when you arrive at school. I will put the photos and stories on the classroom door so that we all can share in the learning. You do not need to return the homework sticker chart; it is for you to keep. Please let me know if you have any questions.

Mrs. Lohmann

Go for a nature walk	Pick apples in an orchard	Go to a corn maze	Go to a pumpkin patch	Dress up like a scarecrow
Make up a story about pumpkins	Make leaf prints with paint	Sort leaves by shape, size, and color	Bake and eat pumpkin seeds	Make homemade applesauce
Line up pumpkins based on size	Drink hot apple cider	Recite "One, Two Leaves Fell Down"	Sing "Ten Little Leaves"	Sing "Five Little Pumpkins"
Read *Fall Leaves Fall!*	Read *It's Pumpkin Time!*	Read *Scarecrow Pete*	Read *Too Many Pumpkins*	Read *Red Leaf, Yellow Leaf*

PLAN BEHAVIOR INTERVENTIONS TOGETHER

The above strategies are important for building relationships with all parents at the Tier 1 level of PBIS. Young children with challenging behaviors will receive supports in Tiers 1 and 2 (and possibly Tier 3). As you design interventions to support young children, I highly recommend including families and other caregivers in the design. Ask parents for their advice on what works for their child. Just remember that some behavior interventions that are used in the home setting are not appropriate for school. For example, a common consequence for throwing a tantrum at home is for a child to be sent to their room for quiet time alone. However, in the school setting, we cannot leave a child in a room unsupervised, so this intervention (or something similar) would not be appropriate for your classroom.

4:1 RULE

When working with families and other caregivers, it is especially important to emphasize the positive. I highly recommend using the 4:1 guideline when working with parents. For every negative or every concern you take to a parent/guardian, you should be sure to share at least four positives. You do not necessarily need to share the positives at the same time as negatives, but it would help to include at least one good thing when you present concerns to parents. And, when possible, I like to sandwich the negative (or the concern) between two positives. For example, I might call Mr. Smith and say, "Hello, Mr. Smith. I hope you are having a great day. I want to make you aware of an incident that happened today. First, I want to tell you that Alejandro did an excellent job of choosing his free play center without assistance. He chose the block center and was doing a great job of building a tall tower. When another child joined him, the child stole one of Alejandro's blocks. Alenjandro looked at the child and yelled 'mine'; I was so proud of him for using his words! When the child did not give back the block, Alejandro picked up another block and hit the child in the head three times. The hitting stopped as soon as I reached the block center. Once I arrived, Alejandro immediately stopped hitting and asked the other child if he was okay. I am proud that Alejandro realized that his classmate might be hurt. He then proceeded to share his blocks with the other child without issues for the rest of free play time. I would like to partner with you to help Alejandro as he learns to play with others. At school we will role-play appropriate play and will reward Alejandro with praise when he shares with other children. I will stay in communication with you about how things are going and would appreciate it if you would talk to Alejandro about sharing and reinforce what we are doing at school in his interactions with his brother at home."

INVITE FAMILIES TO YOUR CLASSROOM

If you are like me, you would prefer to do your own thing and be left alone. We like to leave our classroom doors closed and excel on our own. We have a system and a plan for success but fear that having other adults in the classroom may disrupt that. To best support children and families, though, we need to open up our classrooms and invite other adults to become active participants. In particular, I recommend having an open-door policy and welcoming families in your classroom at all times. Often we are good about inviting families to attend parties and visit for special occasions. These family interactions are wonderful, but they are not enough. Having parents in your classroom for story times, art projects, lunch, or just free play can be a special treat for children and help parents feel more connected to their children's learning. I know of a preschool teacher who invites parents to conduct the fifteen-minute story time at the end of each school day. Each day, a parent volunteers to read books to the class just before pickup. The teacher spends that time cleaning up the classroom and writing notes to parents. Because this volunteer opportunity only requires the parent to arrive fifteen minutes early for pickup, it feels manageable, even for the working parents. In addition, it helps parents feel more connected to the classroom, it is a special treat for the children, and it provides the teacher a brief opportunity to get a few things done. While it may not be realistic for parents to read stories every day, especially if you teach in a full-day center where parents do not all pick up children at the same time, think about other ways can you invite parents to be involved in your classroom.

BARRIERS TO WORKING WITH FAMILIES

While it is in the best interests of children for families and schools to work together, this practice can come with challenges you must be prepared to address. Below I list a few challenges that are most commonly given as reasons that parent-school collaboration does not work.

- **Parent denial of behavior challenges.** In some cases, parents may be unwilling to believe that their child has problematic behavior. In these cases, high-quality data will make a huge difference as you can show the parent the concerns. If you have not realized it by now, I *love* data! By tracking the concerning behaviors, you can prove to the parent that the problem really does exist. In some cases, it may also be necessary to provide video proof of the behaviors, but if you choose to do this, I highly recommend that you video only the specific child to ensure the confidentiality of the other children in the classroom.

- **Previous negative experiences with schools/teachers.** Even by preschool, some parents have already had negative experiences with schools and teachers. These may be experiences they had as parents or as students themselves. Memories of these negative experiences make some parents nervous about teaming with teachers. When it appears this might be the case, I recommend taking it slow and remaining as positive as possible in your interactions with parents. Earlier I mentioned the 4:1 rule. When it appears that parents have had negative experiences with schools in the past, I recommend adjusting this rule to 8:1. In addition, when you discuss challenging behaviors with these parents, be sure that you present a plan for addressing the challenge; come with solutions instead of just problems. Finally, in every conversation with the parent, emphasize the positives about the child. Over time you will likely gain their trust and build a working relationship, but it will require significant work on your part.

- **Work schedules/limited available time.** Today's parents are very busy, and many parents work long days or take work home in the evenings. You will likely have some parents who do not answer your phone calls and do not complete the "homework" you create. When working with busy parents, I caution you not to judge them. It can be very easy to think that they do not care about their children, but this is simply not the case. They care very deeply about their children, and it is likely that their long work hours are one way they are trying to provide the very best for their children. For busy parents, I recommend that you continue providing opportunities to collaborate and communicate frequently. Even if the parents do not respond to your emails, phone calls, and text messages, there is still a very high likelihood that they are reading everything you send them and appreciate the information you are providing. Unless they tell you differently, keep providing information. It is also important that you do not become offended if the parent asks you to communicate less or gives you guidelines on communications that are most important to them. When I taught toddlers, one of the mothers in my classroom was an ER nurse. Our school policy was to call parents any time a child got hurt, even for small injuries. I called the mother one day because her son fell and had a goose egg on his forehead. The mother thanked me for calling and then told me that in the future she only wanted a phone call if it was a major injury that required her to pick him up from school immediately. Otherwise, she could wait until pickup time to learn about injuries. While the other parents in the room still preferred to hear about injuries as soon as they happened, being sensitive to the communication wishes of this mother helped to strengthen our relationship and improved the communications we had.

- **Language barriers.** You are likely to teach children whose primary language is not English. Even if you speak two (or even three) languages, there is still a good chance that you will one day have a child in your classroom whose family speaks a language that you don't. When that happens, you may have trouble communicating with them. If possible, I recommend hiring an interpreter to ensure that your message gets to the parents. If you do not have the funding to hire someone, you can consider using an online translator such as Google Translate, Bing Translator, or Babel Fish. Keep in mind that these programs are not 100 percent accurate, so you will still have some communication barriers. In addition to translation, it can build trust if you learn a few phrases in the family's home language. Even just learning to say "hello" and "thank you" to parents will help build their trust in you. For additional ideas for communicating with parents, see the section on culture in chapter 3.

- **Parents who view teachers as experts.** While we know that teaming with parents is best practice and leads to the best outcomes for students, some parents feel ill-equipped to support the education and development of their children. Parents may believe that teachers are more knowledgeable about teaching, learning, and addressing behavior. In some cultures, the expectation is that parents step back and trust the expertise of teachers. When the parents in your classroom seem to have this perception, it is still important to try to engage in partnership. Your collaboration may need to begin with you providing information about children's development to the parents. Share ideas for how they can interact with and teach their own child (such as the homework calendar), provide paper copies or web links to articles about young children, and talk about what you know about their child. Show your expertise, but be sure to emphasize over and over that you are the expert on education and they are the experts on their child, so you need to work together to get the best results.

MOVING FORWARD

Thank you for sticking with me through four chapters now. I hope that you are beginning to realize that you are already using many best practices in your classroom. PBIS, especially the Level 1 strategies that are considered critical at all levels, are often also considered important for success in the early childhood classroom. Keep working hard and building solid, collaborative relationships with families. I will see you in chapter 5 to discuss building relationships with children.

CHAPTER 5

Tier 1 Intervention: Relationships with Students

Ms. Ahn loves teaching preschool, and one of her very favorite times of each day is when the children walk in the door each morning. Every student has a special hug or handshake that is reserved only for them. The children get so excited to say good morning to Ms. Ahn using their "secret" greeting. All of the children, except for one, run into the classroom each morning and look for Ms. Ahn in order to start this routine. Ralph, on the other hand, walks into the classroom each morning and goes in the opposite direction from Ms. Ahn. Each morning, Ms. Ahn must seek out Ralph and ask him to tell her good morning. While Ms. Ahn feels a strong bond with each of the other children in the classroom, she just can't seem to connect with Ralph. Ms. Ahn decides to find a way to better connect with Ralph, so she begins to sit down next to him during free play time each day and starts a conversation. Over time she learns that Ralph is uncomfortable with touch due to previous physical abuse in this home, and the "secret greetings" scared him. She works with Ralph to develop a no-touch greeting just for Ralph. As the days pass, Ms. Ahn notices that her relationship with Ralph is improving.

RELATIONSHIPS MATTER

More and more, we are learning that relationships between teachers and children are critical for success. When young children have a positive relationship with their teacher, they tend to like school better, are more cooperative, and are more self-directed in their play and interactions (Nur et al. 2018). In addition, strong relationships between teachers and young children increase academic engagement and language skills and reduce challenging behaviors, especially for boys (Van Craeyevelt et al. 2017; Williford et al. 2017). Conversely, young children who have a negative relationship with their teacher tend to avoid school, have trouble participating, and do not adjust well to the classroom setting (Nur et al. 2018). Clearly, building strong, positive relationships with the children in your classroom is not a choice. For children like Ralph, teachers must take the time to make a connection with the child. Your investment in these relationships matters a lot!

START BEFORE YOU EVEN MEET THE CHILD

In chapter 4, we talked about the need to begin building relationships with families before the school year even starts or before a child enters your classroom. Likewise, you should start to connect with the children in your classroom before they become your students. As I mentioned in the last chapter, you might consider sending letters to parents and postcards to children. Getting mail is a very special experience for young children, and I can guarantee that they will be giddy at receiving something from their teacher. Keep the postcard very simple, but also use it as a way to start a conversation with your future students. To make the postcard experience more interactive, you can include a blank self-addressed postcard with the letter to the parents and request that children draw you a picture of something (examples might include drawings of their families, pets, favorite toy, or something they did over the summer). In addition, you can help children become more familiar with you and the preschool by designing your own postcards with a photo of yourself and the front of the school or your classroom. An example of a postcard from a teacher is below.

Dear Raúl,

My name is Mrs. L, and I am so excited to be your teacher this year! We are going to have such a great time together. In our classroom, we are going to do lots of fun things like paint, build with blocks, read stories, cook, and ride tricycles. I also want to make sure that we spend plenty of time doing your favorite things, but I don't know what you like to do. I put a blank card in the letter that I sent to your home. Can you please draw me a picture of your favorite toy or your favorite activity? Once you have made the picture, you can put the card in your mailbox, and the postal worker will bring it to my classroom for me to read. After I read your card, I am going to put it on the bulletin board with the cards from all of your classmates so that I can look at it every day.

I am so excited that you are going to be in my class, and I cannot wait until our first day of school on August 15! Have a fantastic rest of the summer.

Love,

Mrs. L

WELCOME CHILDREN INTO YOUR CLASSROOM

Building relationships with young children can best happen when children feel accepted and comfortable in your classroom. As you design your classroom, think of how you can make it feel like a welcome place for children and for adults. Early in my career, I taught in a school where the principal loved to quilt. Handmade quilts hung in the hallways throughout the building. Between the quilts hung children's artwork and other learning projects. Every day that I walked into that building, I felt like I was home. It felt safe and warm (and that wasn't just because we were in Houston and it was 100 degrees outside!). As a young teacher, I immediately felt welcome in that school, and I know that children and families felt the same way. Think about how you can help children feel like this when they enter your classroom. What can you say to children, and how can you arrange and decorate the room? One thing that helps in many classrooms is to highlight each child through an "About Me" poster and to hang up artwork and photos of the children throughout the classroom. If you choose to ask parents to create a poster about their child, be sure that you collect all of the posters before hanging any up and that you create one for children whose parents do not. Being the only child without a poster would be a sure way to make a child feel unwelcome in your classroom.

CREATE SPECIAL MORNING ROUTINES

Like Ms. Ahn at the beginning of the chapter, you can help children feel welcomed into your classroom through routines that begin the moment they walk into the classroom. I don't know about you, but I love when teaching videos pop up on my Facebook or Twitter feeds, and I can't resist taking the time to watch them. Seeing positive interactions between teachers and children always makes me smile and gets me even more excited about being a teacher. Recently there have been a plethora of videos that show special ways teachers are welcoming children into their classroom each day. From secret handshakes to a menu of ways to be welcomed, teachers are becoming more and more creative. The result is that young children feel welcome when they arrive in the classroom every morning. As you think of ways you can say good morning to the children in your classroom, I urge you to check out a few of the videos in the table for inspiration (some of the videos include older children, but the same strategies can be used in the preschool or kindergarten classroom).

VIDEO	VIDEO NAME AND WEB LINK	THOUGHTS ON THIS IDEA
Secret Handshake	"Teacher Has Personalized Handshakes with Every Single One of His Students" From *Good Morning America*, YouTube Channel www.youtube.com /watch?v=I0jgcyfC2r8	For young children, keep the handshakes simple. As they create their own handshake, they will be tempted to make it long and complicated. Guide them in keeping it simple at first so they can remember it. You can always add to it later.
Choose Your Own Greeting	"Kids Choose Own Greeting to Start School Day" From T&T Creative Media, YouTube channel www.youtube.com /watch?v=Pum938T14Hs	I love this idea of letting children choose how to be greeted every morning, but you should be sure that the greeter also has a choice. I recommend allowing them to create their own menu of ways they are willing to greet classmates.
Good Morning Song	"Using a Song to Learn Students' Names" From Teach for Life, YouTube channel www.youtube.com /watch?v=oDseNz6bzeM	This song can be a great morning routine and a fantastic way for children to learn one another's names. Be sure to vary the order in which you sing each child's name so that the same child is not always first while another is always last.

LEARN ABOUT THE CHILDREN

As the school year begins, take time to get to know each child as an individual. Learn about their interests, their fears, and what makes them anxious or scared. It can be a bit overwhelming to keep track of what you learn, especially if you have a larger class or teach separate morning and afternoon preschool classes. In those cases, I suggest making a simple form for yourself to keep track of what you know about each child—you can use appendixes E and F or create something different. Include things the child says, things you notice, and important information from parents or other adults. I caution you, though, to take concerns from other teachers with a grain of salt. If Zeke had a challenging year with Mr. Phiri last year, do not automatically assume that this year will be challenging too. If Mr. Phiri tells you that Zeke is "a problem" and "always misbehaving," thank him politely for the information, but do not write it down. Rather, resolve to make up your own mind about Zeke. You may find that your experiences with Zeke are much different from those of Mr. Phiri. As you learn more and more about each child, you will find ways to connect with them, discover interests that can be used to enhance learning, and gain knowledge in the many areas in which they need your support and guidance as they grow and develop.

CELEBRATE WHAT MAKES THEM UNIQUE

Once you have learned about the children in your classroom, take time to celebrate them! You can do this in a variety of ways. You can celebrate their birthdays and the most important holidays in their religion or culture. You can plan learning units around their favorite activities or interests (how many of you have a dinosaur or princess theme almost every year because children are so excited about those topics?). You can learn about the activities they enjoy and strike up conversations about those things. If Rafael really likes *PJ Masks*, take some time to watch a few episodes, and then talk with him about the show. Just be sure that your conversation is authentic. Too often our conversations with young children are not reflective of how people actually interact with one another. Frequently we talk to young children about their interests in a manner that focuses more on learning and less on relationship building. For example, I observed a teacher on the playground; a child came up to him and showed him a big red leaf she found. The child was very excited about the leaf, but instead of simply listening to the child, the teacher asked questions about shape, color, and other defining attributes. Soon the child walked away to collect more leaves and did not show them to the teacher. I suspect that if the teacher had asked questions like "What do you like about this leaf?" or "What are you going to do with this cool leaf?" instead of trying to make it into a moment of instruction, the child would have continued bringing leaves to show the teacher.

As you talk to children, remember that they are learning about appropriate conversations in these interactions with you and that using communications to build relationships will lead to better learning over the course of the school year. As you think about how to talk to children about their interests, use the sample conversation below as a guide.

> The entire class is sitting at the snack table. Mr. Rossi begins a conversation with Rafael.
>
> MR. ROSSI: Hey, Rafael. Guess what I watched on TV last night. I bet you will never guess!
>
> RAFAEL: The news? All grown-ups like to watch the news!
>
> MR. ROSSI: Nope! Not the news. Guess again.
>
> RAFAEL: Hmm . . . Well, my dad really likes *NCIS*. Did you watch *NCIS*, Mr. Rossi?
>
> MR. ROSSI: Wrong again. I will give you two clues. You like this TV show, and you told me about it during snack yesterday.
>
> RAFAEL: Mr. Rossi . . . did you watch *PJ Masks*?
>
> MR. ROSSI: I did, and you were right—it is awesome! My favorite part was when Owlette and Gekko got out of the cage and were able to help Catboy save his birthday party. That Night Ninja sure is sneaky!
>
> RAFAEL (*laughing*): I love that one, Mr. Rossi! Night Ninja is always sneaky. I don't like him.
>
> MR. ROSSI: Me neither. He is kind of mean. I would not want to be friends with him!
>
> RAFAEL: Me neither. And do you know what else Night Ninja did? He also stole their sports equipment and helped Romeo shrink Catboy. Night Ninja is a meanie!

As you may have noticed, the conversation between Mr. Rossi and Rafael is natural. It does not feel forced; it is reflective of how adults talk to other adults and how children talk to one another. Mr. Rossi approaches the topic by just chatting instead of asking questions. It is clear that Rafael enjoys the conversation. Natural conversations like this will help build stronger relationships with young children.

TAKE TIME TO PLAY

As a teacher, you are incredibly busy! There is a good chance you do not even have time to eat lunch or use the restroom on most days. Trust me—I know that you are doing your best to get it all done and you feel like there will never be enough time in the day. And here I am, about to ask you to do one more thing. But instead of asking for more time, I am just asking you to reallocate the time you have already. A few times per week, use the time during centers or outdoor play to get down on the floor (or ground) and play. Locate a child who is playing alone (or even a group of children) and join their play. Be sure to let them lead, but participate in their play. Participate like a preschooler, not like a teacher (similar to holding a more natural conversation as illustrated above). Dig in the sandbox. Finger paint. Build a block tower and then knock it down. While you are playing, use the time to have one-on-one conversations with the children about their interests, upcoming events, challenges they are having, or any other topic. Because you are on their level, they are going to be more likely to open up to you. I distinctly remember a conversation with a child in my classroom while we colored pictures together at the table. Her parents had recently had another baby, and during the conversation, she shared with me that she did not like her baby brother because he got all of the attention. I then shared with her that I felt the same way when my little sister was born; it just didn't seem fair! I then told her that, over time, I came to like my sister and that big sisters get to be teachers and help younger siblings learn lots of new stuff. That made her smile, and she began to plan all of the things that she was going to teach her baby brother. Over the following weeks, she told me many stories about how she was teaching her baby brother new things. While I had assumed that she likely felt some jealousy and might have trouble adjusting to a new sibling, I was able to confirm this and help her deal with her feelings because I took time just to be with her. You will be amazed what you can learn during these informal conversations and how many conversations you will have when you take time to play!

FILL THEIR BUCKETS

In an article published by the Center on the Social and Emotional Foundations for Early Learning, the authors use the illustration of a piggy bank as they discuss building relationships (Joseph and Strain 2010). You must put more into the relationship than you take out. You can make "deposits" through spending time with children, engaging in their interests, complimenting them, and making them feel welcome in the classroom. Each time you make a demand of a child or criticize him or her, you are making a "withdrawal" from their piggy bank. It is very important that you make more deposits than withdrawals.

The concept of a piggy bank is similar to that of filling a bucket. In 2006 Carol McCloud published a children's book titled *Have You Filled a Bucket Today?* The gist of this book is that our day (and the days of those around us) will be improved when we fill others' buckets. No, this does not involve taking a sand bucket from the playground and putting stuff inside (although, many children in your classroom will likely enjoy working with you to put sand in a bucket, and spending this time with them will fill their buckets). By doing small things to fill the buckets of the children in your classroom, you can greatly enhance your relationship with them. Look at the list and decide which ones you can do today for each child in your classroom.

IDEAS FOR FILLING THE PIGGY BANKS (OR BUCKETS) OF PRESCHOOLERS AND KINDERGARTNERS

- Smile at them.
- Say hello as they enter the classroom.
- Use children's names when you speak to them.
- Listen to children when they talk.
- Ask questions when children are telling you a story, but be sure that the questions are directly related to the story and are not meant to provide instruction.
- Praise a child (when using praise, be sure that you specifically state the reason for the praise).
- Say positive things about the child to his parents (or other adults) in front of the child.
- Give high fives.
- Play with young children, but let them take the lead in the play.
- For nonnative English speakers, learn some words and phrases in their home language.

If you are anything like me, you like to make to-do lists to check things off and to keep track of your accomplishments. For people like us, on the Bucketfillers 101 website, there is a sheet to help you track your bucket-filling behaviors over the course of a month. You can find it here (or scan the QR code): http://bucketfillers101.com/pdfs/30DayPledgeSheet.pdf.

MOVING FORWARD

Building relationships with young children is hard work and will require significant time and commitment. In the midst of teaching, it may feel like you simply do not have time to do it. But you *need* to make the time. Building a good relationship with some children, particularly those exhibiting challenging behaviors, can feel especially difficult. In reality, though, the "challenging" children often need that relationship with you the most. On the tougher days, remind yourself that you are filling the child's piggy bank so that you can make later withdrawals that will not lead to meltdowns or other challenging behaviors. Now let's head on over to chapter 6 and talk about creating classroom expectations.

CHAPTER 6

Tier 1 Intervention: Classroom Rules and Routines

Ms. Miller has been teaching kindergarten for two years and loves her job. Working with children every day gives her energy and makes her excited for her work. However, some days she is unsure how to guide the children in making the best choices. Ms. Miller relates the story of a recent classroom incident to a friend and asks for her friend's advice. Last week on the playground, the children ran up to Ms. Miller to tell her that they found a hornet's nest. They proceeded to show her where they saw hornets go in and out of a hole in the wood beam on the playground. Ms. Miller instructed the children to stay away from the hornets. A few minutes later, she noticed that the children had their water bottles and were putting water in their mouths and then spitting at the hole in the wood. She quickly went over and reminded the children of the expectation to leave the hornets alone. About five minutes later, she noticed that the children were back by the hornets and were poking the hole in the wood with a big stick. At that point, Ms. Miller decided to end recess. As she relayed the story to her friend, Ms. Miller was clearly frustrated that the students had not followed her instructions and was looking for help. The next day, Ms. Miller began recess by walking with the children over to the hornet's nest and reminding them of the expectations, as well as the consequence (an early end to recess) if they chose not to meet her expectations.

Like Ms. Miller, there are likely times when the children in your classroom do not follow your instructions. Schools and teachers have rules and routines to keep children safe and to help them learn and grow. When children do not follow our rules, it can be frustrating and upsetting. We often turn to a friend to help us better understand what to do. In this chapter, I am ecstatic to be your friend and provide you some advice on classroom rules.

Within the context of PBIS, rules are a critical part of Tier 1. Personally, I prefer the term *expectations* because I think it sounds more positive than *rules*, but you can use either word. You simply cannot have a well-managed classroom without clear expectations. In our daily lives, we encounter various expectations every day. For example, in my job I am expected to grade student papers in a timely manner, complete tasks assigned by my boss without grumbling, and use a professional tone when I speak to both students and colleagues. In my personal life, I am expected to pay bills on time, ensure that my children are fed, and wear shoes when I go to the grocery store. I suspect that your job expectations are similar to mine and that we share at least some of the same expectations in our personal lives. In many ways, our places of employment and our personal lives run smoothly because everyone knows and understands what is expected of them. Similarly, your classroom will run more smoothly if all children and all adults understand what you expect.

WHAT DO YOU WANT?

At the beginning of the chapter, you read about Ms. Miller; her expectations for playground behavior were not being met by the children in her classroom. Before you can begin creating your classroom expectations, you must spend time thinking about what you want. Are you tired yet of me telling you to take time to think before acting? The action-oriented problem solver in me completely understands your annoyance. However, you want to get things right when you implement PBIS, so please take your time. Good, solid plans will lead to good results, and your patience in implementation will pay off in the end.

Appendix H includes a basic form that you can use as you think it through. The left-hand column of the form allows you to list all of the things that you do not want children to do. You will notice that you are asked to list what you want them to do instead in the right-hand column. We refer to these as *alternative behaviors*. It is important that we clarify what we want children to do. When we list only what we don't want, many young children understand what they are not allowed to do but struggle to understand what they should do instead. For example, if I say to Miguel, "No running in the hallways," I may think that I am telling him to walk. However, it is quite possible that he will not understand what I intend. Miguel knows that he is not allowed to run, so he may use a lot of mental energy in thinking about what to do instead. If we could hear Miguel's thoughts, they may go something like this: "Hmm . . . Okay. Mrs. L. does not want me to run in the hallways. I understand that. No more running. But how can I get to the playground if I don't run? What can I do? Hmm . . . Oh, I know! I can skip! Skipping is not running. I think Mrs. L. probably wants me to skip in the hallway." Now, you and I both know that I did not want Miguel to skip. In fact, there is a decent chance that I will now look at him and tell him (in a very exasperated voice), "Miguel. Didn't I just tell you to walk in the hallway? Why are you skipping?" In reality, I did not tell him to walk. He knows that, but he is unlikely to point out my error, or if he does, there is a high likelihood that I will get irritated with him instead of listening to the point he is making. In essence, I will be punishing Miguel when he was trying to follow my rule as he perceived it because I was not clear about my expectations.

So now it is time for you to try this. Open up to appendix H, and then put on your thinking cap. Make a list of all of the things you do not want the children in your classroom to do. Then, for each behavior, list what you want them to do instead. On page 56 you will see an example, but keep in mind that your list will likely be much longer than this. Also, feel free to laugh at some of the things that irritate me (like markers that dry out). I hope that you are encouraged to list those small annoyances as well. While you are making this list, you should write down small annoyances that you want to reduce in your classroom, even ones that do not warrant punishment or consequences for children.

WHAT I DO NOT WANT CHILDREN TO DO	WHAT I WANT THEM TO DO INSTEAD
Run or skip in the hallway	Walk in the hallway
Throw their trash on the floor after snack	Throw their trash in the trash can
Hit classmates when they are frustrated	Use their words
Leave pee in the toilet	Flush the toilet
Spread germs	Wash hands after using the toilet
Talk when others are talking	Listen when others are talking
Tell lies	Tell the truth
Leave toys on the floor	Clean up after centers time
Touch others during circle time	Keep hands to themselves
Yell or scream	Use an inside voice
Intentionally break toys	Use toys as intended
Leave markers open so ink dries out	Put caps on markers after art
Eat food with dirty hands	Wash hands before snack and lunch
Jump off the monkey bars and get hurt	Use playground equipment as designed

LET'S GET ORGANIZED

Nice work creating a list of things you want children to do! Now take that list and group the items into three to five overarching categories. We will call these our Guidelines for Classroom Success. These categories will become your classroom expectations. By limiting the list to just a few, it is more manageable for children to understand and remember. But don't worry—you can (and should) teach every item from your list that falls under that expectation. I created the categories Respect Others, Respect Property, and Respect Yourself, and you can see how I divided my list between these expectations. As you begin to categorize your expectations, you may find that one category has only one item under it. This is okay, especially for an expectation that you highly value (for example, I often put "honesty" in its own category because it is very important to me). Just make sure that you are able to narrow down your expectations to between three and five categories. In addition, you may find that some expectations fall under multiple categories, and this is also okay.

As you design your Guidelines for Classroom Success, you may choose to start with the three categories I or someone else created, or you may choose to create your own categories. Some other ideas for preschool/kindergarten expectations include the following:

- Be responsible. Be respectful. Be honest.

- Make responsible choices. Make respectful choices. Make safe choices.

- We take care of one another. We take care of our school. We take care of our world.

- I show respect. I am kind. I work hard.

As you choose your expectations, though, remember that cute is nice, but practical is most important. We can make even the most boring rules cute and easy to remember through our instruction. Here's how I grouped my list of expectations into Guidelines for Classroom Success.

RESPECT OTHERS	RESPECT PROPERTY	RESPECT YOURSELF
Walk in the hallway.	Throw trash in the trash can.	Use words.
Use words.	Clean up after centers.	Tell the truth.
Flush the toilet.	Use toys as intended.	Wash hands before snack and lunch.
Wash hands after using the toilet.	Put caps on markers after art.	Use playground equipment as designed.
Listen when others are talking.	Use playground equipment as designed.	
Tell the truth.		
Keep your hands to yourself.		
Use an inside voice.		

Okay, did you finish that? This was a big step in the PBIS planning process, and you have now laid important groundwork for the work that is to come. Go get yourself a treat and take a deep breath. When you are ready, come back to me and we will move to the next step. You are doing wonderfully preparing for PBIS in your classroom, and I am proud of you!

IT'S TIME FOR SOME FUN!

Let's take your three (or five!) categories and make them into your classroom PBIS expectations. This is where we can get creative. I am going to take my three expectations (Respect Others, Respect Property, Respect Myself) and create a preschool-friendly theme with them. Then I will design a poster to show these overarching expectations, but I want to make sure that the poster is both eye appealing and easy for the children (and any adults who come into my classroom) to understand. My classroom poster will play on the letter *R* at the beginning of each of my expectations. I am adding the concept of being a star to make it more appealing to the children and because I can later use this idea to ask the children if they "*R* being a star." Here is my very basic poster. Because I like to keep my classroom materials fun but also not too overwhelming, I keep all of the text in black and then print my poster on a fun color of paper. Alternatively, you can use colorful letters and graphics and print on white paper, but be aware that this could be too overwhelming for children with sensory challenges. As you make your poster, you can use simple tools such as Microsoft Word or web-based programs like Canva and PicMonkey. Remember that fancier does not mean better, so don't stress over making it perfect.

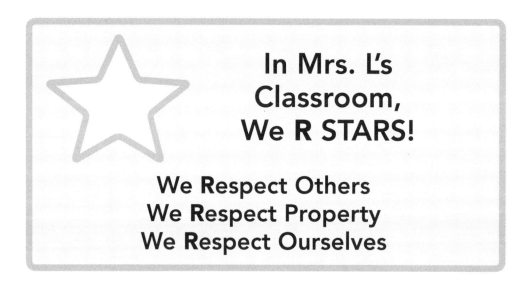

If I did not want to use the concept of stars as outlined above, I could instead refer to my classroom expectations as the "3 *R*s" and use an image of a personified *R* on my poster. However, as I mentioned earlier, I like to keep things simple. Here are some other ideas for making your classroom expectations fun:

- Use the word *bee* instead of *be* and include images of bees on your poster.

- Choose an animal and create the poster to encourage students to "be a lion" (or eagle, or any other animal).

- Use an image of a personified *I* instead of the letter *I*. Many people are tempted to use the image of an eye with the letter *I*, but I recommend against that because it can be confusing to young children.

- Use simple graphics to show a key idea for each expectation.

As you determine the categories and theme you will use, you might be tempted to search online or use social sites such as Pinterest or Teachers Pay Teachers as a guide. These can be great ways to spur your thinking, but be careful that you are searching for ideas that align with what you are learning here in this book. Internet resources can be wonderful and are often very appealing to the eye, but they are not always evidence based. You can choose to use a poster of classroom expectations that you find online, but be choosy when doing so and make sure that it includes the classroom expectations you already decided upon. Do not change your expectations simply because you found a cute poster on Pinterest.

NOW LET'S MAKE A MATRIX

Did you enjoy that? I really hope so. Being creative to enhance children's learning makes me happy, and I like to think that my readers like it too. The poster you created shows your overarching classroom expectations. Now you need to take those expectations and create a matrix that explains how the expectations look in various environments. For example, flushing the toilet is a sign of respecting others in the bathroom, but it is not an expectation in the block center. In the block center, taking turns with the cool tunnel blocks is a sign of respecting others. You will find templates for this matrix in appendix I and a sample completed matrix below. As you fill this out, try to be as specific as possible, as this will guide the next steps in the PBIS implementation process. On page 60 you will find a sample chart that is partially completed to help you begin to think through how to complete this matrix.

	EXPECTATION 1: WE RESPECT OTHERS	EXPECTATION 2: WE RESPECT PROPERTY	EXPECTATION 3: WE RESPECT OURSELVES
Hallways	• We walk. • We whisper. • We walk in a straight line. • We tell the truth.	• We keep our hands at our sides. • We close the classroom door gently when we leave the room. • We avoid walking into walls and other objects in the hallway.	• We think before acting. • We keep trying, even when we make mistakes. • We make choices that keep our own bodies safe.
Playground	• We take turns with toys. • We use kind words. • We tell the truth.	• We use all toys as intended. • We clean up toys when we are done.	• We think before acting. • We keep trying, even when we make mistakes. • We make choices that keep our own bodies safe.
Restroom	• We tell the teacher before going to the restroom. • We flush the toilet after using it. • We tell the teacher if the toilet is clogged. • We tell the teacher if the toilet tissue needs to be refilled. • We give one another privacy when using the toilet. • We wait in line patiently for our turn to use the toilet and to wash our hands. • We use a quiet voice.	• We throw away paper towels after washing our hands. • We use a paper towel to wipe water off the sink. • We tell the teacher if the toilet is clogged. • We use an appropriate amount of toilet tissue to ensure that the toilet stays unclogged.	• We think before acting. • We keep trying, even when we make mistakes. • We make choices that keep our own bodies safe. • We close the door to our toilet stall while we are using it. • We wash our hands with soap after using the toilet. • We use toilet tissue to clean our bottoms or ask a teacher for help when needed. • We make sure that our clothes are back on our bodies properly before leaving the restroom.

As you likely noticed when looking at my matrix, I like to be extremely specific and think of every challenge that is likely to occur in each location. The more specific I can be in this step, the more prepared I will be for proactively addressing these potential problems before they occur. Once I have created this matrix, I am ready to plan for teaching my expectations.

Teaching the children about the content of the poster is important. If you just stick that cool poster you made up on the wall and never mention it to the children, it is pretty likely that they will never see it. It will be a cute addition to your classroom decor, but it will not be functional and it will have no impact on children's behavior. Let's compare it to putting a poster of the alphabet on your classroom wall but never talking to the children about letters. They might notice the poster and might eventually make the connection that they see letters on the wall and in the books they look at in the classroom library, but their understanding of letters and written language will still be very limited if you never talk to the children about letters or explicitly teach them the purpose of written language. You will have a similar result if you put your behavior expectations on the wall but never talk about them. I don't want you to waste all of the hard work you put into making that poster, so let's make a plan for helping children to see, understand, and use what you have created.

To have an impact on young children's behavior, you must explicitly teach your expectations. In many ways, behavior knowledge is like any academic skill. It needs to be taught through the use of intentional instruction that includes evidence-based teaching practices. Because I am pretty old-school when it comes to teaching (and because I know that this format works), I default to using standard lesson-planning templates that begin with evaluating current knowledge, proceed to instruction, include group-guided practice, and end with independent practice. In the preschool or kindergarten classroom, circle time is often the perfect place for providing instruction on classroom expectations. I highly recommend that this instruction begins on the first day of the school year or whenever a new child enters your classroom. When you first begin teaching the expectations, you should present all three to five overarching expectations and then spend time specifically teaching what each one looks like in a variety of locations and situations (that is, in each of the boxes in your matrix). Keep in mind that this is a lot of material to teach and this instruction will take a *long* time to do well. Plan for this instruction on classroom expectations to take at least a couple of weeks. On pages 62–67, I provide a sample lesson plan that can be used to teach the first box in my matrix (respecting others in the hallway). You will notice that I like to script my lesson plans. Please note that this is not necessary, but it does help many teachers (like me) to think through exactly what to say before they teach a lesson. Because teaching can be unpredictable, there is no guarantee that the lesson will go just as planned, but having a specific guide helps many teachers feel more prepared. You may also note that this is a long lesson and it might be challenging for some young children to sit still for more than a few minutes. I have used this lesson successfully when I make funny voices for the puppets, but if your students need a shorter lesson, you can break this into two or three smaller lessons and tell the story over a few days. Make the adjustments needed to ensure success for your students.

RESPECTING OTHERS IN THE HALLWAY

Lesson taught during circle time on day two of school year

LEARNING OBJECTIVE
Young children will understand the expectations for behavior in school hallways and be able to exhibit desired behavior in the school hallways with at least 80 percent proficiency with fewer than two teacher prompts per student.

MATERIALS NEEDED
Classroom Expectations poster
Puppets—Sam Sheep, Greta Goat, and Francisco Farmer
Finger puppets—2 for each child
Lines of masking tape along the floor (one line per child)

LESSON LENGTH
20 minutes

INTRODUCTION
The teacher will ask the children if they remember the classroom expectations that were presented the day before. Using the poster to guide the discussion, the class will discuss the three classroom expectations. Then they will practice reciting them, first as a group. After stating each expectation once together, each child will turn to the child sitting next to them, and they will say the first expectation together three times. The first time they say the expectation, the pair should be standing up. The second time, they should be hopping on one foot. The final time they say the expectation, they should have their eyes closed and be touching their noses. After saying the expectation all three times with their partners, children should sit down. When all children are seated, the teacher will say "Hmm . . . Thanks to all of your good memories, I now know that we respect others in this classroom. But I am wondering what that means. Let's find out together."

EXPLICIT INSTRUCTION

TEACHER: Okay, class. It is time for us to learn about respecting others. But I know that this is a very big thing to learn, so today we are just going to talk about what it means to respect others in the hallway. Class, please point to the hallway.

CHILDREN *point to hallway.*

TEACHER: Thank you! You are correct. That is the hallway. Who can tell me where we might go if we are walking in the hallway?

CHILDREN *answer. Possible answers might include going to the playground, other classrooms, and the restroom; coming to school and going home after school.*

TEACHER: Those are great answers! We have to go in the hallway to get to a lot of places! Because we are going to be in the hallway every day, I think it is really important that we know how to do it correctly. To help us learn what it means to respect others in the hallway, I have brought my special friends, Sam Sheep and Greta Goat. Everyone say hello to Sam and Greta.

CHILDREN: Hello, Sam and Greta.

SAM SHEEP: Well, hello children. I am so excited to be here today. And I am really happy that I get to help you learn to respect others. Did you know that *respect* is one of my favorite words?

GRETA GOAT: Wow, Sam. You must be very smart. You know some very big words. I don't know what it means to respect. How do you know so much?

SAM SHEEP: Well, thank you, Greta, for the kind words. I think you are very smart too. Would you like me to help you learn about respect? I am just about to talk to these wonderful children about the word. You can join us.

GRETA GOAT: Oh, could I? Yes, Sam, please!

SAM SHEEP: Okay, Greta. Let's get started. So, the word *respect* means that we treat people kindly because we care about them.

GRETA GOAT: Oh, I understand that. So maybe we give them cookies? Everybody loves cookies!

SAM SHEEP: Yes, Greta, we could give them cookies. But even more important, we can do things that show we are thinking of them and that we care about them. We show respect through our actions. Let's pretend that we are going to the playground now.

GRETA GOAT: Oh, I love the playground! The slide is my favorite. Don't you just love the slide, Sam? Don't you, don't you?

SAM SHEEP: Yes, Greta, I do. But did you know that when you just interrupted me, it did not show respect?

GRETA GOAT (*putting her hand over her mouth*): Oh no! I am so sorry, Sam. Can you forgive me?

SAM SHEEP: Of course, I can, Greta. We are friends! But now I would really appreciate it if you would listen for a minute.

GRETA GOAT: Okay, Sam. I can do that.

SAM SHEEP: Let's pretend we are walking to the playground. We can pretend that this line of tape on the floor is the hallway and we need to walk from this end, which is our classroom, to the other end, which is the playground. Let's walk together, Greta.

Sam and Greta begin walking on the line. After a few steps, Sam starts to run and spin in circles. He bumps into Greta several times while spinning but keeps running and spinning.

GRETA GOAT: Sam, what are you doing? That is really loud when you run. And you just ran into me. That hurt. Please stop!

SAM SHEEP: Wait? You did not like it when I bumped into you? Why not?

GRETA GOAT: Well, because it hurt. And it made it hard for me to walk.

SAM SHEEP: Okay, so you are saying that I did not respect you by touching you and keeping you from walking? Is that right?

GRETA GOAT: Yes, Sam, yes. You told me that respecting someone means that we show that we care about them. When you bumped into me on purpose, it made me think you did not care about me.

SAM SHEEP: I am sorry, Greta. You are right. I was not showing that I care about you, and I was not being respectful. Okay, let's try this again.

Sam and Greta go back to the "classroom" end of the tape and begin walking. This time they walk side by side all the way to the end.

GRETA GOAT: Sam, Sam, did you see? Did you see? We did it! We used our walking feet when we went to the playground, and we were respectful! Yay!

SAM SHEEP: You are right, Greta. We did! Good for us! (*Sam pauses and appears to be thinking*) Uh-oh. I just thought of something. What if Clementine Cow wanted to walk from the playground to the classroom while we were using our walking feet to get to the playground? There would not have been space for her to go past us.

GRETA GOAT: Oh no! You are right. And if we did not make space for Clementine, we would not be showing her respect. I have an idea, Sam. What if you walk in the front and I walk behind you? Then there will be lots of room for Clementine too.

SAM SHEEP: That is a great idea. Let's try it.

Sam and Greta start walking with Sam in front and Greta behind.

SAM SHEEP (*yelling while walking*): Greta, Greta . . . can you hear me? Can you hear me? Greta? Greta?

GRETA GOAT (*yelling while walking*): Sam? Sam? I can hear you. Can you hear me? Isn't this great, Sam. Isn't it great? We are being so respectful! Yay for us!

Francisco Farmer pops up.

FRANCISCO FARMER: Sam and Greta . . . what are you doing? You are being so loud. It is very hard for my class to listen to a story because you are being so loud. Can you please be a little quieter?

SAM SHEEP: We weren't being loud. I think you must be thinking of someone else. We weren't even talking.

FRANCISCO FARMER: Sam, that is not true. I know that you and Greta were being loud. You just lied to me. When you tell a lie, you are showing the other person that you do not respect them enough to be honest.

SAM SHEEP (*gasping*): Oh no! I do respect you, Francisco Farmer. I am sorry that I told a lie. You are right. We were being loud in the hallway. I am sorry that we were loud and even sorrier that I told a lie.

FRANCISCO FARMER: Thank you for being honest and for apologizing, Sam. I know that you respect me, and I respect you too.

GRETA GOAT: We are sorry, Francisco, for being loud. We will be quieter.

FRANCISCO FARMER: Thank you, Sam and Greta.

Francisco Farmer disappears.

GRETA GOAT (*in a whisper*): Gosh, Sam. I feel so bad. We were not very respectful of Francisco Farmer when we were yelling. I think we should be quiet in the hallway. Maybe we should just whisper or not even talk at all.

SAM SHEEP: I think you are right, Greta. Thanks for thinking of this.

Sam Sheep and Greta Goat continue walking toward the playground.

SAM SHEEP (*once they reach the playground*): Great work, Greta! We were respectful in the hallway. We walked instead of running or spinning. We made a line so that people could go past us. We told the truth. And we used quiet voices to show respect to Francisco Farmer.

TEACHER *sets down Sam and Greta.*

TEACHER: Class, can anyone tell me what Sam and Greta learned?

CHILDREN *answer. Possible answers might include being quiet in the hallway, walking in a line, walking instead of running or spinning, or telling the truth.*

TEACHER: You are right! And because we **R** stars, we are going to practice what Sam and Greta learned to show respect to those around us. We know that showing respect means that when we are in the hallway, we walk, we whisper or stay silent, we stay in a line so that people can pass us, and we always tell the truth. Now I am going to ask you some questions, and I want you to tell me if the person is showing respect to others in the hallway. Are you ready?

CHILDREN *respond.*

TEACHER: Clementine Cow wants to take a ball to the playground, so she runs to the classroom to get one. Is she showing respect to others? If you think she is showing respect, stand up on one foot. If you think she is not showing respect, jump.

CHILDREN *jump.*

TEACHER: Great answer! You are correct. If Clementine is running in the hallway, she is not showing respect to others. Let's try another one. Horatio Horse is so excited about going to the playground. He has a great idea for a new game and he cannot wait to tell Sam Sheep all about it. Horatio holds his hand over his mouth so that he can stay quiet while he walks down the hall. Is Horatio showing respect to others? If you think he is showing respect, pat your tummy. If you think he is not showing respect, pat your head.

CHILDREN *pat their stomachs.*

TEACHER: Excellent work and good listening! You all really understand the idea of showing respect to others.

GUIDED PRACTICE

TEACHER: Okay, now that we have seen Sam Sheep and Greta Goat walk in the hallway and we have talked about examples of being respectful, I think we should try to do it. Show me a thumbs-up if you are ready to try this.

CHILDREN *give teacher a thumbs-up.*

TEACHER: We are going to pretend that our classroom is the hallway. Let's get into a line. I will be the line leader. Before we start, can you please remind me what we should do while we walk in the hallway?

CHILDREN *answer. Possible answers include walking, being quiet, staying in a line, and being honest.*

TEACHER: Great answers. It sounds like you are ready. Let's walk!

TEACHER *begins walking and children follow behind her. While walking, teacher provides feedback as necessary to children, both praise and correction. After two laps around the classroom, teacher stops walking and children also stop.*

TEACHER: Great work! I noticed that you stayed in line, you used walking feet, and you used your quiet voices. I am proud of you for showing respect to others while we practiced walking in the hallway.

INDEPENDENT PRACTICE

TEACHER: You all did a great job of walking around the classroom. I am very impressed that you used your walking feet, stayed in a straight line behind me, and whispered. You are very good at this! Now let's see if you can help our puppets show respect to others in the hallway. Each of you should choose two puppets and find a line of tape on the floor.

CHILDREN *choose puppets and find a line of tape. The teacher should help children to ensure that everyone has a tape line of their own.*

TEACHER: Thank you for getting your puppets and finding a line of tape. Now I would like you to help your puppets get from one end of your hallway to the other while showing respect for others. When they get to the end of the hallway, they should turn around and do it again. Ready, set, go!

CHILDREN *have puppets walk, one in front of the other, on the lines of tape. During the activity, the teacher walks around the classroom to assist children as needed. Practice continues until all children are able to successfully help their puppets show respect while walking.*

TEACHER: Nice work helping your puppets learn to show respect in the hallway. Please put the puppets away, get your coats, and line up at the door.

ASSESSMENT

TEACHER: Thank you for putting away your puppets and lining up so quickly. Now we get to practice what we learned today. We are going to the playground. Let's show everyone that we know how to show respect to others in the hallway. Remember, that means that we will be quiet, stay in line, and use our walking feet. Let's go!

The teacher and the children walk from the classroom to the playground, with the teacher at the front of the line. While they walk, the teacher will evaluate the children's behavior and provide individualized feedback as necessary.

CONCLUSION

Upon reaching the playground, the teacher should gather all of the children around her.

TEACHER: Practicing what we learned was really fun! How do you think you did at respecting others in the hallway? Give me a thumbs-up or thumbs-down.

CHILDREN respond, likely with thumbs-up.

TEACHER (*only if children respond with thumbs-down or there were challenges in the hallway*): Our walk in the hallway did not go quite as planned. What do you think we should do to improve when we walk back to the classroom after playing?

TEACHER should allow children to respond.

TEACHER (*if children respond with thumbs-up and the teacher agrees that they met the expectation of respecting others in the hallway*): I think you did a fantastic job of showing respect to others while we walked in the hallway. You were quiet, walked, and stayed in line. I can't wait to do that again after playing outside. But now, it is time to play!

REFLECTING ON THE LESSON PLAN

As you look at the sample lesson plan, you may notice several things. First, you may notice that the teacher repeats the specific actions that constitute respect for others in the hallway over and over again. As you read the lesson plan, it might have almost felt annoying to you to hear the same thing repeatedly. However, we know that children learn best through repetition. Repeating the phrases "quiet," "walking feet," and "walk in line" over and over will help children truly understand what you expect from them.

Second, you likely noticed that the teacher uses a variety of ways to present the idea to the children. First, she has puppets demonstrate the skill. Then she has the children respond to examples and nonexamples. Next the entire class practices the expectations together in the classroom. After that the children help puppets practice the skill. Finally, the teacher leads the class in practicing the expectations by actually walking in the hallway. Through every step of the lesson, the teacher ensures that students are engaged and they understand what is being taught. The teacher provides feedback to help students better internalize the concept. The feedback provided should include validation that children are providing the correct answers and gentle guidance when they provide incorrect answers. One way to provide gentle guidance is to praise the child for answering and then ask a question that will lead to the correct answer. For example, if Freddy answered that we use the hallway to get to the block center, I might say, "That is a very good answer, Freddy. You are correct that we must walk to get to the block center, but we don't need to use the hallway to get there. Can you think of a place we go that requires us to leave the classroom and use the hallway?"

Does this lesson plan process sound familiar? I certainly hope so. I suspect you have noticed that this lesson plan is similar in structure to the lesson plans you might use to teach letter sounds, counting skills, or basic science concepts. This is because we should teach behavior skills and expectations in the same ways that we teach any academic skill. Lesson plans that are focused on behavioral expectations should look very similar to any other lesson plans you write.

Finally, you likely noticed that this lesson plan addresses only one small box in the matrix. By breaking down your overall classroom expectations into small lessons based on each box, the children in your classroom will have an easier time learning what you expect. This process will take longer than teaching everything at once but will be more effective.

WHAT IS YOUR ROUTINE?

In addition to teaching our classroom expectations, it is also important to teach children what we expect during the daily classroom routines. Making your classroom run smoothly requires predictable and intentional routines. In all likelihood, those routines are going to be very different from the ones the children have in their own homes, so you will need to teach them what you want them to do at certain times of the day. But first you will need to think about exactly what your routines are and what you expect from children. Appendix J will help you as you think this through. On page 69 I have provided a partially completed routine planning sheet to help you begin thinking about your own routines.

TIME OF DAY/ACTIVITY	ROUTINE EXPECTATIONS
Arriving in the classroom	1. Children hang up their jackets and backpacks in their cubbies. 2. Children put their lunch boxes in the red tub by the table. 3. Children put their water bottles in the blue tub by the table. 4. Children choose an activity from the options on the independent work bookshelf and then sit down at the table to complete it. 5. If children complete one activity, they may put it away and get a new one. 6. Children continue working on independent work until circle time.
Coming to circle time	1. When children are called to circle time, they quietly put away independent work. 2. Children find their carpet square that has been placed in the circle time area and sit on their square. 3. Children are quiet while waiting for others to arrive at circle time.

By looking at the table, you can see that I have very specific expectations about what I want the children to do. When children first become your students, *you* know exactly what you expect when children arrive at school and when they go to circle time. However, *they* do not know. If the children are new to school, this might be their first experience with set routines, and even if they attended preschool or other out-of-home care before, the teacher likely had different expectations than you do. To help them understand your expectations during routines, you will need to directly teach those routines. To do this, you will use the same methods you used to teach the classroom expectations. You will create a lesson plan that includes teaching the skill as well as multiple opportunities for the children to practice the routine, both as a group and individually. Throughout the practice, you will provide feedback. As needed throughout the year, you will reteach and review the classroom routines.

MANAGING EXPECTATIONS AND ROUTINES

Nice job teaching the children in your classroom what you expect from them! By now, they know your classroom expectations and what those look like in a variety of settings. In addition, they have learned your routines throughout the school day. However, like all people (adults included), they are going to need reminders sometimes. I recommend that you take a few minutes of circle time every single Monday morning (and every morning for the first week back after any school break of one week or more) to review the expectations. Get your puppets out and have the children and the puppets practice meeting the expectations. Remember that we don't teach children the alphabet on the first day of the school year and expect them to know it all year long. We reteach it and review it throughout the school year. We need to do the same thing with behavior skills.

In addition, as you prepare for PBIS in your classroom (and especially once you begin implementing it), you need to ensure that all adults who spend time working in your classroom know your expectations. They must have the exact same expectations for behavior any time they are working with the children in your classroom. This means that you will need to take time to train all floaters and substitutes about PBIS and how it looks in your classroom. This is extremely important, as consistency significantly increases the likelihood that children will be successful. They never have to wonder what the expectations are when the rules are the same with every single adult.

MOVING FORWARD

Congratulations! We are now about halfway done with this book. You have done a lot of hard work in planning your PBIS system. Now comes the fun part as you get to implement interventions and see children succeed in meeting behavioral expectations. I am very proud of you for sticking with me so far. I know that this process has not been easy, but I promise it will be worth it. Go reward yourself for creating posters and lesson plans and for teaching both adults and children your classroom expectations. Put your feet up, grab your favorite beverage, and have a TV binge or a bubble bath. I will see you soon in chapter 7!

CHAPTER 7

Bridging beyond Tier 1 Intervention: Examining Instruction

Diego is a very bright five-year-old in Mr. Deepak's classroom. Whenever Mr. Deepak teaches a lesson, Diego seems to understand the concept very quickly. He is always the first child in the classroom to finish activities and never seems to make a mistake in his work. While Mr. Deepak is very impressed that Diego seems to learn so quickly, he has noticed that Diego often gets into trouble during review lessons or when Mr. Deepak is helping struggling learners. It seems to Mr. Deepak that Diego is looking for something to keep himself entertained when he has already learned the material, and that throwing toys and pulling other children's pigtails are his chosen means of entertainment. Mr. Deepak is at a loss for how to manage Diego's behaviors while still teaching the other children in the classroom.

Like Mr. Deepak, you have done a great job preparing the children in your classroom for meeting expectations and providing them feedback on how they are doing. For the most part, the children are probably doing what you want and things are running pretty smoothly in your classroom. However, things are not perfect and there are some behavior challenges. In fact, there is a fairly good chance that you are currently wondering if PBIS really works or if you have wasted a lot of time. Rest assured that this is normal. Tier 1 PBIS is awesome, but it will not prevent everything. As we discussed in chapter 2, having a solid Tier 1 will ensure that about 85 percent of children do what's expected most of the time. Tier 1 will prevent most behaviors, but alone it is not enough. Some children will need more.

When you notice that a child (or a group of children) is struggling in your classroom, the first step is self-reflection. You need to take some time to consider what you are doing that might cause (or reward) the behavior. The magic formula for changing children's behaviors is to change adult behaviors. And, as a teacher, the very first behavior you should consider is your instruction. Before you create behavior interventions or individualized programs for children with behavior challenges, I highly recommend that you take some time to truly examine your instruction. You may be able to solve the behavior problems by just tweaking your lessons a bit (and wouldn't it be cool to fix a problem that quickly?).

As a general rule, when we teach, we create lessons and activities that meet the needs of the "average" child. Of course, we know there is no such thing as an "average" child, as every student in your classroom is different. But we still do tend to design activities and lessons based on the learning needs of most children in the classroom. We sometimes forget that what works for one child (or group of children) may not work for everyone in the room. While Johnny, Suzie, Carlos, and Tamako all love to paint and will happily spend hours working on art projects for each holiday, Jamal spends just a few minutes working on the project before moving to a more physically active activity. And while Jamal learns the words and actions to songs after seeing and hearing them just once, Suzie needs to observe you for several days in a row before she is ready to try singing. As you read this, I suspect you are nodding your head. You see this in your classroom every single day. Each child is different, and our classroom instruction needs to reflect this. So, let's chat about how to do this.

REFLECTING ON YOUR TEACHING

Close your eyes and think about one lesson or activity you taught today. I suggest thinking about circle time, as that is often the point in the day when we work on new concepts and all children participate. Think about the goals of the lesson, the activities you included, the engagement level of the children, what worked, what did not work, any challenges you faced, particularly with behavior, and what you might do differently next time. Keep your eyes closed for as long as you need. Don't feel bad if you doze off for a few minutes—we teachers are tired and should take any opportunity we can to get a little rest. Just be sure that when you wake up, you get back to work.

After you have had time to reflect on the lesson, turn to appendix K: Lesson Reflection. Using the information you just considered (before and after your nap), answer the questions. I have provided a completed sample form. If it is reasonable within your schedule, I recommend that you complete this form for at least one lesson per day for an entire week. This will help you look for trends. Remember that as long as you are using it to improve instruction, more data is always a good thing— and you know how much I love data!

1. What was the topic of my lesson?
   Counting objects to ten

2. What was the learning objective?
   By the end of the lesson, each child will be able to independently count ten objects with at least 80 percent accuracy and no more than one prompt.

3. What activities did my lesson include to achieve that learning objective?
   Read *Ten Apples Up on Top*
   Counted felt apples that fell from the apple tree on our felt board
   Jumped ten times while counting our jumps
   Counted as a group the number of children in the circle (there were ten)
   Counted our fingers as a group
   Sang "Ten Little Children"
   Children independently glued ten paper apples on paper.

4. Which children seemed engaged in the lesson?
   Alex, Kamal, Sarai, Kishan, Rachel, Matthew, Padma

5. Which children did not seem engaged in the lesson?
   Fiona, Madeline, Ziyad

6. Were there certain activities that seemed more engaging for children? If so, which ones?
   Singing, felt board, jumping, gluing apples onto paper

7. Which children met the learning objective?
   Alex, Kishan, Rachel, Matthew, Padma, Fiona

8. Which children did not meet the learning objective?
   Kamal, Sarai, Madeline, Ziyad

9. What went well in the lesson?
    Group counting
    All children participated in the song.
    Most of the children met the learning objective.

10. What challenges occurred during the lesson, including behaviors?
    After jumping, Madeline had a hard time calming down and stopping jumping.
    Instead of gluing the apples on the paper, Fiona threw them at Sarai. She did
        complete the project when I sat next to her and kept her on task.
    During the story, Fiona was poking Kamal and Rachel (they were sitting on either
        side of her).
    During the story, Madeline kept wiggling and kicking her legs.
    Kamal, Sarai, Madeline, and Ziyad were unable to count ten apples to glue onto
        their papers.

11. Which children had behavior challenges?
    Madeline, Fiona, Kamal

12. What is my hypothesis for why those particular challenges occurred?
    Maybe Madeline needs more movement.
    Maybe Fiona was bored.
    Maybe Kamal was irritated about being poked.
    Maybe Kamal, Sarai, and Madeline do not fully comprehend the concept of counting
        to ten.
    Ziyad threw up after lunch and went home sick—maybe he does not understand
        counting or maybe he was just feeling poorly.

13. What would I do differently if I taught the lesson again?
    I wonder if this lesson would be better taught in small groups.
    I wonder if more movement would help.

As you looked at my completed appendix K, I suspect that you were nodding your
head and laughing as you thought about very similar situations in your own classroom. I imagine that you have taught a lesson very similar to this before—a great
lesson with fun activities that works well for most children but not for all of them. So
let's talk about what to do now. As I mentioned earlier, completing this form for several days and comparing the information to look for trends will help you get a better
idea of what is going on. If I continued this process for a full week, I might have
discovered that Fiona always has behavior problems during math lessons and that
Madeline appears to be more focused after physical activity. I might also discover

that after staying home sick for two days, Zayid came back to school and was able to count to ten without any prompts. After collecting information for a few days, my answers to question 13 might be much longer and more in-depth. If you plan to complete this form for several days, it is okay to leave that final question blank and return to it when you can look at all of the data together and be more thorough.

MEETING THEM WHERE THEY ARE

As you probably noticed in my example, the children in a classroom are likely at different learning levels and have a variety of needs during a lesson. When the lesson is not ideal for a child, they have a higher likelihood of misbehavior. Because you know the children in your classroom well, you likely have a good idea of what they need and about their individual levels of learning and development. You can also consider the data from assessments such as HighScope, GOLD by Teaching Strategies, and the Desired Results Developmental Profile—Kindergarten. Or, you can create your own assessment forms to track children's progress and learning. All that matters is that you think about the needs of each child and how those needs affect learning and behavior. When it comes to behavior, several common mismatches between instruction and student needs lead to behavior problems. These include children who have already mastered the content, children who are struggling to learn the content, children who need extra movement, and activities that are not engaging to children.

SUPPORTING ALL LEARNERS THOUGH UDL

As you consider how to meet the needs of the children in your classroom, I highly recommend considering the Universal Design for Learning (UDL) framework. We don't have time to thoroughly discuss UDL here (and, if I tried, this book would be twice as long), but here is a quick overview. UDL is based on the idea that all learners are different and we should design instruction that prepares for the diversity in our classroom. We do this through the use of multiple means of engagement, multiple means of representation, and multiple means of action and expression. Basically, this means that we use children's individual interests to get them excited about learning, teach with a variety of strategies, and have children show us what they know in multiple ways. Using the UDL framework in your preschool classroom will help reduce behavior challenges by supporting you in matching the instruction to children's learning needs. The table lists a few useful online resources for learning more about UDL, especially in early childhood classrooms.

RESOURCE	AUTHOR(S)	WEBSITE
"About Universal Design for Learning"	CAST	www.cast.org/impact/universal-design-for-learning-udl
"The UDL Guidelines"	CAST	http://udlguidelines.cast.org
"Universal Design for Learning (UDL)"	Early Childhood Technical Assistance Center	http://ectacenter.org/topics/atech/udl.asp
"Using a Universal Design for Learning Framework to Enhance Engagement in the Early Childhood Classroom"	Marla J. Lohmann, Katrina A. Hovey, and Ariane N. Gauvreau	http://josea.info/archives/vol7no2/vol7no2-5-FT.pdf
"Using a Universal Design for Learning Framework to Provide Multiple Means of Representation in the Early Childhood Classroom"	Ariane N. Gauvreau, Marla J. Lohmann, and Katrina A. Hovey	https://scholarworks.lib.csusb.edu/cgi/viewcontentcgi?article=1083+context=josea

FOR THOSE WHO NEED A CHALLENGE

Diego from Mr. Deepak's classroom at the beginning of this chapter and Fiona from the completed appendix K provide excellent examples of children who cause behavior problems due to boredom. Both of these children may need an additional challenge in order to be successful in your classroom. It is clear that Fiona has already mastered the skill of counting to ten. She was able to achieve the lesson objective before the lesson even started. Some children who already know the topic being taught are content to sit and participate in the activities. But other children, like Fiona, are not. Because they already know the subject, the lesson is boring to them. This causes these children to look for something to entertain themselves. Often this "something" is manifested in the form of behavior challenges. It is likely that Fiona was poking other children and throwing apples just to keep herself busy. For children like Fiona, we need to provide challenge within the lesson so they do not have time to get bored. Because Fiona already knows how to count to ten, I should consider providing a different lesson objective for her. For example, instead of teaching her to count to ten, it might be appropriate to help Fiona learn to count to twenty. To support her in doing this, I would ask her to count every child in the room twice (to get to a total of twenty), count her fingers and toes, and put twenty apples on her paper. If I did not want to ask Fiona to count higher, I could instead have her work on patterns or sorting within the counting activities. For example, she would need to figure out how many boys and girls are in the classroom or glue the apples on her paper by alternating red and yellow apples. She would still need to participate in the group lesson and listen to the book, sing the song, and jump with us. However, providing even a little bit more challenge may help Fiona stay more focused and reduce her challenging behaviors.

Coming up with ideas for appropriate lesson modifications, especially on the spot, can be difficult, so I recommend thinking about the skills you will be teaching later in the school year. Is Fiona ready for what is normally taught next month? Is she ready to try the lesson objectives that are normally taught in six months or next year? Use your school's learning scope and sequence to identify future lesson topics that might be appropriate for Fiona.

FOR THOSE WHO NEED MORE SUPPORT

While some children need extra challenge to be successful, other children may need additional learning support. It is very likely that you will have one or two children in your classroom who struggle to keep up with the rest of the students when learning new skills. Even at a young age, children do not want to be known by their peers as "the dumb one" and would prefer to be known as "the class clown" or even "the bully." Because of this, it is common for young children who learn at a slower rate to have behavior challenges. When teachers ensure that the lesson provides a way for every child to succeed, struggling learners are more likely to focus on learning instead of on misbehaving.

By looking at appendix K above, we can see that four students did not meet the lesson learning objectives. Based on the other information provided, we can surmise that Ziyad's illness prevented him from learning and that Madeline might need more movement to be successful (we will talk about how to help her later in this chapter). We also see that Kamal and Sarai were unable to count to ten by the end of the lesson, and nothing else that was noted on the form provides an explanation for this. It is possible that these two students may need extra support to learn math concepts. For struggling learners, we may need to adjust expectations just as we do for children needing more of a challenge.

For struggling learners, the first thing we will want to do is to identify their learning needs. We can do this through making notes based on our observations and looking at our assessment data. This should give us a solid understanding of each child's learning level. Next we will want to consider if this learning level is developmentally appropriate. Remember that young children develop at various rates and learn new concepts at different speeds, so it is likely that Kamal and Sarai are doing just fine developmentally. However, if you have concerns that a child is not developing appropriately, I highly recommend that you talk to your director or principal and consider a referral for a developmental assessment from the school district special education department.

Once you have determined Kamal's and Sarai's learning levels, you can make adjustments to the lesson to support their needs. Let's assume that an appropriate lesson objective for Kamal is to learn to count to seven and that Sarai can be expected to count to five. Both children will still need to be fully included in the lesson and activities (and should not be separated from the rest of the children in any way). But you will need to modify instruction for them so they can be successful. For example, it is okay for both of them to stop counting and to stop jumping once they have reached five or seven, and you will not call on either of them to count in front of the other children for any number above four or five. Finally, you can adjust the independent work for each child. You could ask Kamal to put seven apples on his paper and Sarai to put five on hers. Or you could scaffold their learning to get to ten apples. To do this, you might choose to draw ten circles on their papers and ask them to glue one apple per circle. Or you could draw three circles on Kamal's paper and then ask him to glue on seven apples and then put apples on the additional three circles (to help him get to ten apples total). When finding ways to adapt the instruction, be creative.

As you are thinking about ways to adapt instruction for struggling learners, I highly recommend that you are sensitive to the social impact of any lesson adjustments. For example, if you have Kamal and Sarai glue apples onto yellow pieces of paper, Fiona use brown paper, and the rest of the class use white, children will quickly notice that things are different, and some child will inevitably ask you about the different colors of paper. One alternative to this approach is to write children's names on the papers when you prepare them so that you know who gets which paper. When you are designing instruction, think about how to make all lesson adjustments as inclusive as possible. Using the UDL framework discussed earlier in the chapter will help you do this effectively.

FOR THOSE WHO ARE NOT ENGAGED

If you have determined that a child's misbehavior is not because the content is too easy or too hard, the next thing to consider is whether the child finds the learning interesting. When children are actively participating in learning, they do not have time nor desire to act inappropriately, so increasing children's engagement often reduces behavior challenges.

Just like adults, children tend to stay on task for longer periods of time when they find the activity fun or stimulating in some way. Personally, I can spend hours listening to lectures and presentations from researchers on the topics of classroom instruction and behavior management. Attending education research conferences is one of my favorite hobbies, and I never get bored doing it. However, most people I know would fall asleep or start throwing spitballs during the first presentation of the morning and have a hard time paying attention to an entire day of presentations. I find education research conferences exciting and fun, while others do not. It is like this for children in your classroom too. Some (or maybe even most) of them enjoy your lessons and never seem to get bored, but there are likely a few children who struggle to stay on task. For these children, you need to focus on making learning engaging for them. To do this, I recommend the strategies outlined below.

The first option for increasing children's engagement is to provide choices whenever possible. Young children love to be decision makers and will often get more excited about the activity when they are involved in some portion of the planning. You can provide simple choices like the color of crayon to use, whether to use paint or markers, or whether to sit or stand during circle time. Alternatively, you can (and should) allow children to make choices about how to spend their free time, whom to play with, and what portion of a large project they want to work on first. While it may not be possible to let children make choices about everything that happens in the classroom, even providing small decisions throughout the day will often increase children's engagement and reduce behavior challenges.

A second way to increase children's engagement is to connect learning to their interests. The son of one of my closest friends *loves* dinosaurs (and to be fair, don't most preschoolers love dinosaurs?). He knows the names of virtually every dinosaur that has been discovered and can talk for hours about them. As my friend started to teach him basic math skills, she quickly learned that he was more excited if the activities included dinosaurs. So they counted dinosaurs, sorted dinosaurs by colors and other attributes, and made patterns with dinosaurs. Any time she pulled out the dinosaur toys, her son was excited and happily worked on math for as long as she wanted. Think about ways that you can include children's interests in the lessons. With a classroom full of children, you may have to get creative, and not every child's interests will be represented in every lesson. But it is still worth your effort. Plus, think about how much fun it will be to count tutu-wearing dinosaurs riding motorcycles!

FOR THE WIGGLY ONES

As you think about ensuring that your instruction is appropriate for the children, there is one more consideration. Like Madeline earlier in the chapter, many young children (and adults) are wiggly. If I am completely honest, I don't sit still well and find being forced to sit in a chair and pay attention to be incredibly uncomfortable. I mentioned earlier that I love attending education research conferences, but I rarely sit still while I attend; I wiggle my leg, quietly tap my pen on my leg, or stand at the back of the room for most of the presentations. The truth is that we humans were not made to sit still, and there is quite a bit of research indicating that our brains actually stop functioning as well when we don't move enough. Preschoolers need to move often in order to learn. While increasing movement in your lessons will help all children, it is critical for the success of wiggly kiddos like Madeline. To help her, I recommend thinking about small ways to add move movement to your activities. Here are a few simple ways to add movement to group activities:

- whole-body songs/chants during circle time (examples include "Head, Shoulders, Knees, and Toes" and "The Ants Go Marching")

- marching around the classroom while practicing a skill (this is great for practicing counting or singing the alphabet)

- jumping or hopping on one foot while practicing a skill

- having children change positions every few pages during read-aloud (one example is sitting for three pages, then standing for three pages, and then sitting again)

- allowing children to choose their body position during circle time activities (some children may choose to sit, some may stand, and some may change positions frequently)

- rotating activities during circle time/group lessons so that calm activities are followed by active activities

As a bonus, adding more movement to your classroom instruction also means that you will be getting more exercise into your day. More exercise in your workday will keep you sharper and more on the ball too!

MOVING FORWARD

Once you have ensured that you are meeting the learning needs of all children in your classroom, you can move forward. Like our discussions in the previous chapters, examining your classroom instruction will not solve all behavior issues, but it is one more tool for reducing those challenges. Behavior problems that arise after implementation of a solid Tier 1 (which includes collaboration with families, relationships with children, classroom rules and routines, and strong instruction that matches children's needs) will require specific interventions in Tiers 2 and 3 of the PBIS pyramid. Let's head to chapter 8 to start talking about how to select and prepare for these interventions.

CHAPTER 8

Determining the Purpose of Challenging Behaviors

Mr. Garcia is having a great school year. He is using what he learned about Tier 1 PBIS to create a solid foundation for student success in his classroom. He has been watching Mrs. Smith, who teaches next door. He has noticed that his classroom seems to run more smoothly than hers and that she is dealing with a lot more problem behavior than he is. Mr. Garcia attributes the difference to the solid foundation he has created through Tier 1 PBIS. Despite his success, there are still three children whose behavior worries him, and he is wondering how he can support them now. In particular, he is concerned about Alejandro, who has a habit of yelling when other children touch the toys he wants.

So here we are: chapter 8. Like Mr. Garcia, you have implemented a solid Tier 1 PBIS system in your classroom, and I hope you are seeing success with fewer behavior challenges than in the past. But we are not done yet. In chapter 2, we discussed the PBIS pyramid (as a refresher, you can see the image again here). We talked about the fact that most children will have behavioral success with Tier 1 universal supports. However, a small percentage of children need additional supports that we can provide through Tier 2 small group and easy-to-implement interventions, as well as Tier 3 individualized interventions. There is a very good chance that two or three children in your classroom could use just a little extra help through Tier 2 supports, and there may be one child (hopefully, not more than two) who really need Tier 3 interventions to be successful in your classroom. So let's talk about how to help these children.

Tier 3
Individualized
Interventions

Tier 2
Small-Group Interventions

Tier 1
Universal Prevention Strategies

BEFORE YOU BEGIN

Take a few minutes to think about your classroom and about the children you teach. Jot down on a sticky note the names of the children you believe could use more behavior support. Identifying these children is the first step in planning for Tiers 2 and 3. Implementing Tiers 2 and 3 interventions can be challenging if you jump right in without first planning (and you know how much I value planning).

The behavior interventions you use in Tiers 2 and 3 are not a specific list of ideas that work for every teacher or classroom. Instead, I am going to present you with some potential interventions, but you will have to choose the appropriate one(s) based on the needs of the child and the reasons they are struggling with behavior. Behavior interventions only really work when they are aligned with the behavior itself. So, before we start talking about interventions, we first need to talk about the reasons for behavior.

WHY ARE THEY DOING THAT?

As you are thinking about the children in your classroom, you are likely asking yourself why in the world Sasha uses a high-pitched shriek when she is upset or why Rafael throws a block at you when you do not respond to him immediately. All behavior has a purpose. Behavior specialists call this the *function* of the behavior. Everything we (or children) do, we do for a reason. Those reasons can be summarized into four categories: gaining attention, gaining something tangible, avoiding or escaping something, or fulfilling sensory needs (which includes avoiding something that is too stimulating). When I get up each morning, I pet my puppy to get some love and attention. Then I make coffee to gain something (in most cases, the coffee gives me my sanity!). After breakfast, I brush my teeth so that I can avoid cavities. And I put on fuzzy socks because I love the way they feel on my feet. Every single action I do has a reason. Likewise, every action a child does is also for a reason. If we think about Alejandro from the beginning of the chapter, we can hypothesize that his yelling has the function of gaining something tangible; he is using the yelling to get the toy another child is currently using.

Sometimes we talk about how little children have big emotions and how those emotions dictate their behavior. This is very true, but often those big emotions are caused by the child's desire for something. Sometimes, though, behaviors are caused by emotions and happen because the child is trying to escape or avoid their feelings.

Right now I would like for you to take out a piece of paper and write down ten actions you have completed today. Next to each action, list the function the behavior serves. Remember that your behaviors provide attention, help you get something you want, assist you in avoiding something unpleasant, or meet a sensory need.

Now that you have thought about your own behavior, get a new piece of paper. Choose a child in your classroom but not one of the children you believe needs Tier 2 or 3 interventions. Observe the child for about fifteen minutes and write down five behaviors (acceptable or unacceptable) that you see the child doing. Make a guess as to the purpose of those behaviors. Once you have done this, I recommend that you ask the child to explain to you why they did those certain actions and compare the responses to your guesses. It is okay if you were wrong; this activity is just to get you thinking about children's motivations. It is possible that the child will not know why they do things—this is okay too.

CONDUCTING A BEHAVIOR ASSESSMENT

Next it is time to put your knowledge to work to help the children in your classroom. As always, start small. Choose one child and one behavior (or category of behaviors) that is currently the most problematic for you. If there are any aggressive or harmful behaviors in your classroom (examples might include biting, hitting, kicking, and self-harm), I highly recommend that you target those first. After you have chosen the behavior to target, you need to create a very specific definition of the problematic behavior. Using the most exact terms you can, write down what the child is doing. For example, state that Jin bites other children on the arm, often leaving a mark. Anyone seeing that definition will understand what behavior you are targeting. On the flip side, if you write that Jin "is aggressive," I might think that he throws chairs across the classroom or kicks teachers in the legs. A precise definition for the behavior means that all adults working with the child can be on the same page about the problem and the solution. It will also allow you to take better data on the effectiveness of any interventions you might try. Finally, having a precise definition helps all adults to focus on the behavior itself instead of the child, which reduces the likelihood that adult bias will affect our classroom management decisions.

Now we are going to find the function of that behavior for that particular child. My favorite way to gain a better understanding of a challenging behavior and to determine the function is to observe the behavior and take data (yep, data) on the behavior and the circumstances that surround it. The simplest way to do this is through the use of an A-B-C chart. The *A* stands for *antecedent* and indicates what happened just before the challenging behavior. The *B* is the *behavior*. And the *C* is the *consequence*, which is whatever happened after the behavior. It is important to understand that a consequence can be positive or negative and may be planned or unplanned. Basically, the word *consequence* does not always mean punishment, and in many cases it actually means a reward for the behavior. Earlier we talked about the function of behaviors; the consequence is related to the function, and examining the consequence(s) will aid us in determining the likely function of a child's behavior.

Don't worry if the A-B-C chart doesn't make sense yet. We are going to work through this together. Let's use the example of Jin from earlier in this section. Through my behavior definition, I identified that Jin bites other children on the arm and leaves a mark. For the safety of all children in the classroom and for Jin's social development, this clearly must be addressed quickly. To better understand Jin's behavior, I will need to work on an A-B-C chart for as long as necessary to get useful data and make a guess about the purpose of Jin's biting behavior. In all likelihood,

I can do this in a week or so (and even faster if Jin bites frequently). If possible, I should record every single time that I observe the behavior, but this is not always realistic, so it is okay to fill out the chart based on random occurrences of the behavior. If you choose to record only some behavioral instances, though, remember that your data is incomplete, so there is a chance that you may be missing a piece to the puzzle. With that being said, some data is better than no data, so I encourage you to do what is most feasible in your classroom.

LET'S TRY THIS TOGETHER

On pages 88–89 you will see a completed A-B-C chart. You will notice that there are four columns; please note that the first column is optional and you may choose not to use it. I include it on the chart because it can be beneficial to understand when and where the challenging behavior occurs. However, as you are first learning to assess behavior, you should keep the process as simple as possible and focus your attention on the other three columns.

As you are completing this chart, it is important that you stick to the facts only, precisely what you observed happening; do not include your opinions or interpretations of what you observe. In addition, and if time allows, I suggest completing an identical chart for another child in the classroom whom you do not perceive as having challenging behavior. Sometimes when we take data on two students, we realize that the behavior is actually an issue for many children, but we may not have noticed it for others. Taking this data helps us to reduce the chance of bias toward one child or group of children. Research over the past few decades has indicated that preschool boys of color are more likely to be identified as having problematic behaviors than are their classmates (Meek and Gilliam 2016). As teachers, we must be cognizant of this trend and cognizant of our own biases to ensure this does not occur in our own classrooms. One way to avoid bias is by taking extra data to compare the children we believe need Tiers 2 and 3 interventions and other children in the classroom.

RESOURCES FOR LEARNING ABOUT BIAS IN THE CLASSROOM

- Katie Kissinger, *Anti-bias Education in the Early Childhood Classroom: Hand in Hand, Step by Step* (New York: Routledge, 2017).

- Louise Derman-Sparks and Julie Olsen Edwards, *Anti-bias Education for Young Children and Ourselves*, 2nd ed. (Washington, DC: NAEYC, 2019).

- "Understanding Anti-bias Education," NAEYC, www.naeyc.org/resources/pubs/yc/nov2019/understanding-anti-bias.

DATE/TIME/ LOCATION	ANTECEDENT	BEHAVIOR	CONSEQUENCE
Monday, March 4 9:30 a.m. Block center	Jin and Sarah were the only children playing in the block center during centers time. Sarah had the blue half-moon-shaped block in her left hand. Jin tried to take it out of her hand. Sarah pulled her arm back and held on to the block.	Jin leaned over and bit Sarah on the left arm, leaving teeth marks.	Sarah dropped the block and started screaming. Jin picked up the block and started to play with it. Ms. Santos went over to Sarah, hugged her, put ice on her arm, and invited Sarah to read a book with her. Ms. Santos made Jin leave the block center and play alone in the transportation center.
Tuesday, March 5 3:15 p.m. Group time/art project	The entire class was at the table, painting pictures of flowers. Jin was sitting on the end, and Raúl was to his left. The container of blue paint was sitting in front of Jin. Raúl reached over, with his right arm, and grabbed the blue paint.	Jin leaned down and bit Raúl on the right arm, leaving teeth marks.	Raúl dropped the blue paint and started crying. The paint went all over the table, the art projects, the floor, and got on Raúl and Jin. Ms. Santos went over to Raúl, hugged him, put ice on his arm, and asked him to go with her to change into clean clothes. Ms. Santos made Jin leave the table and go to the bathroom to change clothes. The art activity ended because all of the pictures had blue paint on them. After helping Raúl, Ms. Santos cleaned up the blue paint.
Wednesday, March 6 1:30 p.m. Library center	The children were finishing up their naps and going to the library center for quiet reading after waking up. When Jin awoke, he went to the library center and sat down next to Kamal. Kamal was reading *Little Blue Truck*.	Jin leaned over and bit Kamal on the right arm, leaving teeth marks, and grabbed the book from Kamal's hands.	Kamal grabbed another book and hit Jin on the head. Both boys started crying. Ms. Santos went over and hugged both boys and then offered them both ice for their owies and a chance to sit on her lap while she read *Little Blue Truck* to them.

DATE/TIME/ LOCATION	ANTECEDENT	BEHAVIOR	CONSEQUENCE
Wednesday, March 6 4:00 p.m. Playground	Andrew was riding the blue tricycle on the sidewalk around the playground. Andrew stopped at the stop sign. Jin was standing next to the sign.	Jin grabbed Andrew's left arm and pulled it to his mouth. Jin bit Andrew's arm, leaving teeth marks. Then, Jin pushed Andrew off the tricycle.	Jin got onto the tricycle and rode around the playground. Andrew lay on the ground, crying, until Ms. Santos came over and helped him up. Ms. Santos took Andrew inside to clean up the dirt from his fall and to put ice on his arm. Ms. Santos and Andrew were inside for about ten minutes while the other teachers on the playground watched all the children. When Ms. Santos returned to the playground, she made Jin give the tricycle back to Andrew and then made Jin sit next to her for a few minutes.
Thursday, March 7 8:00 a.m. Circle time	All of the children were asked to grab a spot and take it to the carpet for circle time. Jin was standing in line behind Kamal to get a spot. Kamal picked up the blue spot, smiled at Jin, and started to walk away.	Jin grabbed the blue spot out of Kamal's left hand and bit Kamal on the left arm.	Kamal began to cry. Jin took the blue spot to the circle time carpet and sat down on it. Miss Julie hugged Kamal and put ice on his arm. Then, Ms. Santos asked Kamal to sit next to her and be her special helper for circle time.
Friday, March 8 9:30 a.m. Transportation center	Jin, Henrik, and Samuel were playing in the transportation center. Jin had the blue car and Henrik had the red train. Samuel had the orange car. He told Jin, "I want the blue car. You have the orange car," and attempted to pull the blue car out of Jin's hand.	Jin leaned down and bit Samuel on the right arm, leaving teeth marks.	Samuel began to cry while Jin continued playing with the blue car. Ms. Santos came over and put ice on Samuel's arm. Then, she took the blue car away from Jin and told Jin that she needed his help to put away all of the blue naptime mats.

As you looked at the chart, you may have noticed that the teacher reported only the facts and avoided subjective statements like "Jin looked frustrated" or "Kamal was irritating Jin." At this point, you should report only exactly what you observe and avoid making assumptions about children's feelings or motivations. Reading that chart may have evoked several emotions in you. I imagine you might have laughed a bit at the chaos that ensued in the classroom, nodded your head in understanding because you have had very similar days, wanted to cry for all of the children with bite marks on their arms, and felt annoyed at the teacher for allowing Jin to hurt so many children. I also bet you began to notice a pretty clear pattern as you looked at the A-B-C data. Before the behavior, another child had something that Jin wanted, or another child was trying to take something that Jin had. While one could argue that the other children's actions may have been wrong or disrespectful, at this point, we are focused on Jin's biting behavior. Also, as a side note, you may also have noticed that everything Jin wanted was blue. Knowing that information may help you create interventions later, but for now, let's just focus on Jin's responses. Jin responded to the situation by biting another child on the arm in each of the six recorded instances. And in five out of the six instances, Jin got the desired item for at least a short period of time—the only exception to this was the paint because it spilled and was no longer usable. Jin's biting behavior worked to get the object he desired. Based on this data, we can assume that the function of Jin's behavior was gaining something. While I included data from only one week, which may seem very short, the data is pretty strong and provides us with good evidence to make a guess about the purpose of Jin's behavior. Therefore, we do not need to keep collecting this data any longer. At this point, we can begin formulating a plan to help Jin and protect his classmates' arms. In later chapters, I will share specific strategies that can be used to address challenging behaviors. For Jin, I would suggest explicitly teaching him how to respond to challenging behaviors and providing rewards when he responds appropriately.

LET'S TRY ANOTHER ONE

That example was pretty easy, so let's try another one. In this scenario, Ms. Santos has identified that Sahana exhibits several behaviors that can be defined as aggressive, but she is currently unable to provide a behavioral definition that is common for all of the behaviors. Ms. Santos has decided to complete an A-B-C chart to help herself think about the behaviors she is seeing.

DATE/TIME/ LOCATION	ANTECEDENT	BEHAVIOR	CONSEQUENCE
Monday, March 11 8:00 a.m. Circle time	The entire class was seated at circle time while Ms. Santos read a story. Sahana was seated between Kamal and Jin.	Sahana leaned over to Jin and used the palm of her left hand to hit him on the back of the head.	Ms. Santos reminded Sahana that "in our classroom, we keep our hands on our own bodies" and then told Sahana that she needed to sit by Ms. Santos for the rest of circle time.
Monday, March 11 9:45 a.m. Dramatic play center	Sahana was playing with Sarah in the dramatic play center. The girls were putting on costumes and looking at themselves in the mirror.	Sahana yelled (in a very loud voice), "Ms. Santos, Ms. Santos, come quick, come quick!" Almost immediately, Sahana started throwing hats out of the dramatic play center, and the hats hit other children on the head.	Ms. Santos ran to the dramatic play center with the belief that something must be wrong (her initial thought was that maybe there was a bee in the hats). When Ms. Santos arrived, Sahana said, "Don't we look beautiful? We are princesses!" Ms. Santos complimented the girls on their outfits and then told them about her favorite dress-up clothes from childhood.
Monday, March 11 10:15 a.m. Playground	Sahana was playing in the sandbox with several other children. They each had a bucket and a shovel and were building sandcastles.	Sahana lifted her bucket over Andrew's head and poured the sand on his head. Then, she hit Andrew in the head with her shovel.	Andrew started screaming and crying. Ms. Santos and Mr. Garcia both ran to the sandbox. Mr. Garcia picked up Andrew and took him inside to help him get the sand out of his eyes and off his body. Ms. Santos put her hands on her hips and (in a very loud voice) told Sahana to get out of the sandbox and come with her. Ms. Santos took Sahana to the bench and told her to sit down. Then she sat next to her and explained to her that "we do not hurt our friends, and it hurt Andrew's body when you put sand on his head." Sahana sat next to Ms. Santos for the rest of outside time.

DATE/TIME/ LOCATION	ANTECEDENT	BEHAVIOR	CONSEQUENCE
Monday, March 11 11:00 a.m. Group time	All of the children were sitting at the table, working on lacing cards. Ms. Santos was sitting next to Jin and talking to him about his blue whale lacing card. Sahana was seated at the other end of the table.	Sahana took the string out of her lacing card and wrapped it around Sarah's neck.	Sarah started to scream, and the other children quickly alerted Ms. Santos about what was happening. Ms. Santos moved her chair to the opposite end of the table and sat next to Sahana. Ms. Santos said, "Sahana, it appears that you are having a hard time being kind today. I will have to sit right next to you in order to help you make the right choices."
Monday, March 11 12:10 p.m. Lunch table	The class was seated at the table having lunch. Sahana was sitting between Raúl and Ara, eating. When lunch began, all of the children were eating quietly, so Ms. Santos took the opportunity to go and lay out the naptime mats.	Sahana threw her placemat across the room, hitting Ms. Santos in the leg.	Ms. Santos returned the placemat to the table and sat down in an empty chair across from Sahana. She stayed at the table and spent the rest of the lunchtime talking to Sahana and the other children about the behavior expectations at the lunch table.
Monday, March 11 3:30 p.m. Art center	Sahana was working independently in the art center, making a collage of flowers to give to her mom. She had been in the art center for about ten minutes while Ms. Santos was reading stories in the library center.	Sahana picked up the bottle of liquid glue and turned it over, dumping it out on the floor. Then, she yelled, "Ms. Santos! The glue spilled! I need HELP!"	Ms. Santos grabbed a roll of paper towels and went over to the art center. Together Sahana and Ms. Santos cleaned up the mess. Once it was cleaned up, Sahana joined the children in the library center and listened to stories.

This second A-B-C chart is less obvious than the previous one, but a thorough inspection of the Consequences column reveals that every behavior incident resulted in attention from Ms. Santos. While most of us view being lectured or having to sit next to the teacher as a negative experience, for some children any attention is a special reward. These children would rather have negative attention than no attention at all. Based on the information we can see regarding Sahana's aggressive behaviors, we can assume that she is seeking attention from Ms. Santos. There is a good chance that her behaviors may also have a second underlying reason, but we will focus on just one function of the behavior at a time and start with the most obvious. In this case, attention from the teacher is the most obvious behavior function. You likely also noticed on this A-B-C chart that all of the instances occurred within the same day. While it is normally best practice to take data over several days, here there was enough data to make a tentative behavior plan, as long as Ms. Santos was willing to revisit that plan if it did not work.

A-B-C CHARTS IN YOUR CLASSROOM

As you look at my completed A-B-C charts, you will notice that I included a narrative in each section. In fact, if you read the three sections in succession, it sounds like a story. This is intentional. The more details you provide, the better understanding you will gain of the behavior and the higher the likelihood that you will be able to remember the incident accurately later. Just remember, though, that as you tell the story on the A-B-C chart, you need to be an unbiased observer and avoid any judgment or speculation; just report the facts. You cannot have too much information on this form, but I caution you to be realistic. Don't try to put in so much information that this process takes you considerable time to complete after each behavior incident—you could miss out on valuable instructional time for all children (or worse yet, you could be so busy completing the form that you miss seeing other behavior challenges).

I have included a blank A-B-C chart in appendix L for your use. In addition, I have created a similar form in appendix M, but it uses more user-friendly terms and is ideal for data collection by other adults in your classroom who may not understand the behavior terminology.

If you are nervous about trying to use a behavior chart and making a mistake in your analysis, I recommend practicing a bit in a no-pressure environment. You can complete an A-B-C chart on your dog's barking or on the Three Stooges hitting one another on the head (there are many clips online that are perfect for this practice).

MOVING FORWARD

Once you have had time to do a little behavior assessment and think you have a solid understanding of the behavior of one child in your classroom (remember that we are starting small and supporting one child first), move on to chapter 9. In that chapter, we will talk about creating a plan for addressing the behavior and using data to ensure that your plan is working. I am excited to get to talk to you about data again! I will see you in chapter 9.

CHAPTER 9

Creating a Behavior Plan

Ms. Santos has completed the A-B-C charts for the two children who concern her the most, Jin and Sahana. She feels pretty confident that Jin bites other children to gain (or keep) something he wants and that Sahana engages in challenging behaviors to get her attention. Armed with this information, she is ready to support both children by developing personalized behavior plans that use evidence-based interventions and are feasible to implement in her busy classroom.

After your hard work in chapter 8, you now have at least an idea of the observable reasons the children in your classroom are showing challenging behaviors. You will use this information to create a behavior plan that supports the unique needs of each child. Before you create this plan, you will need to read chapters 10 and 11 and learn about the specific behavior interventions you can try. As you choose a behavior intervention, you should ensure that the intervention matches the function of the behavior. To help you do this, I have created the chart below with the four functions of behavior and interventions to match. You will notice that most—but not all—of the interventions can be used to support a variety of causes of behavior.

INTERVENTIONS FOR CHILDREN WHO WANT ATTENTION

- Behavior-specific praise (chapter 10)
- Time-out from the activity (chapter 10)
- Nonverbal cues (chapter 10)

- Visual reminders and cues (chapter 10)

- Providing choice (chapter 10)

- Pre-correction statements (chapter 10)

- Teaching new skills (chapter 11)

- Teaching replacement behaviors (chapter 11)

- Individualized visual cues (chapter 11)

- Behavior contracts (chapter 11)

INTERVENTIONS FOR CHILDREN WHO WANT TO GET SOMETHING

- Redirection/distraction (chapter 10)

- Removal of the problem-causing item (chapter 10)

- Time-out from the activity (chapter 10)

- Nonverbal cues (chapter 10)

- Visual reminders and cues (chapter 10)

- Providing choice (chapter 10)

- Pre-correction statements (chapter 10)

- Rewards (chapter 11)

- Teaching new skills (chapter 11)

- Teaching replacement behaviors (chapter 11)

- Individualized visual cues (chapter 11)

- Behavior contracts (chapter 11)

INTERVENTIONS FOR CHILDREN WHO WANT TO AVOID OR ESCAPE SOMETHING

- Removal of the problem-causing item (chapter 10)

- Time-out from the activity (chapter 10)

- Nonverbal cues (chapter 10)

- Visual reminders and cues (chapter 10)

- Providing choice (chapter 10)

- Pre-correction statements (chapter 10)

- Structured breaks (chapter 11)

- Teaching new skills (chapter 11)

- Teaching replacement behaviors (chapter 11)

- Individualized visual cues (chapter 11)

- Behavior contracts (chapter 11)

INTERVENTIONS FOR CHILDREN WHO HAVE A SENSORY NEED

- Time-out from the activity (chapter 10): this can be used when the child is overstimulated

- Nonverbal cues (chapter 10)

- Visual reminders and cues (chapter 10)

- Sensory tools (chapter 11)

- Structured breaks (chapter 11)

- Teaching new skills (chapter 11)

- Teaching replacement behaviors (chapter 11)

- Individualized visual cues (chapter 11)

- Behavior contracts (chapter 11)

CHOOSING AN APPROPRIATE INTERVENTION

Let's chat about how you should choose an intervention or two to support a child or group of children. First, you will want to make sure that the intervention matches the behavior. If Ms. Santos were to provide Sahana with a sensory tool each time she engaged in a challenging behavior, it is unlikely that her behaviors would improve.

Second, you need to make sure that the intervention(s) you are choosing are feasible within your classroom setting and that you (and all adults working in your classroom) are willing to do the intervention without fail. If you know that you have too many competing demands, choose a simpler intervention. If the thought of finding clip art to create visual cues sounds overwhelming, try a different intervention first. Or, if you know that the floater who covers your classroom during your lunch break refuses to use rewards for individual children, you will want to consider other interventions.

Next you want to consider the appropriateness of the intervention for the child. Not all interventions will work for all children. If you have already been using one of the listed interventions with fidelity (that means as intended and every single time the behavior occurs), but it is not working, it is likely not appropriate for this particular child at this time. If the child does not like to be touched, you will not want to use praise in the form of a high five.

A LITTLE BASELINE DATA

While you are making a decision about an intervention or two to try, you will need to take some baseline data. This means that you will need to gain an understanding of either how often the behavior occurs or how long the behavior lasts (tracking the length of the behavior is most common for temper tantrums). Having baseline data will give you some basic information about how problematic the behavior truly is. In addition, you will use this baseline data to compare to the data you are taking during the intervention. Having data about the behavior before trying an intervention will help you know whether your behavior plan is actually working for the child.

To track how often the particular behavior occurs, you will use a frequency count. That is a fancy way to say that you will keep track of how many times the behavior occurs during a certain time span. At some point, you will need to record the frequency on the official form, but carrying a piece of paper or a clipboard with you all day long can be a challenge. So I recommend using a simple method to track the frequency throughout the day and then recording it at the end of the day or during breaks/downtimes. Here are a few of my favorite methods for tracking frequency in the midst of a crazy day:

- Wear either an apron with pockets or a carpenter's belt. Put a handful of beads or beans (or any other small objects) in the left-side pocket. For each instance of the behavior, move one object to the right-side pocket. At the end of the day or time period, count the objects in your right-side pocket and record that number.

- Tie a string of beads tightly on your wrist. The string should only be about one-quarter full with beads. For each instance of the behavior, move one bead from the outside of your wrist to the inside. At the end of the time period, count the beads on the inside of your wrist and record that number.

- Put hair ties or rubber bands on your left wrist. Every time the behavior occurs, move one hair tie/rubber band to your right wrist. When the time period is over, count and record the number of hair ties on your right wrist.

- Keep a small sticky note and a pen in your pocket. Make a tally mark each time you observe the behavior. When you get the chance, record your data on the official frequency tracking form.

Below and on page 100, you can see examples of two frequency recording forms. One is very basic and includes only morning and afternoon. The second form lists specific time intervals. These forms can be found as appendix N (the basic form, which is intended to be used over the course of a week) and appendix O (including time intervals, which will require a new form each day). Appendix P provides a third option for you to create the rows in a way that works best for you.

BEHAVIOR TRACKING FORM

Child: Jin
Behavior: Biting

DATE	MORNING	AFTERNOON	NOTES
February 26	1	2	Morning: block center Afternoon: playground (both times)
February 27	1	0	Morning: circle time Jin left school just before lunch for his annual well exam and did not return
February 28	3	2	Morning: block center, art table, playground Afternoon: playground, group table work
March 1	0	0	
March 2	1	3	Morning: transportation center Afternoon: classroom library, doing puzzles at table, playground

The basic time interval chart above shows the frequency with which Jin bit a peer over the course of a week. Since this behavior only happens a few times per day, the basic frequency chart is the most appropriate. By looking at this data, we can see that Jin is not any more likely to bite a peer during any certain part of the day. You will notice that the far-right column provides a place for the teacher to make notes. For infrequent behaviors, I like to write down location or antecedent to help me look for a pattern (with Jin, I noticed that most of the biting instances happened during less-structured activities). This column is also the ideal place to note anything abnormal that might have happened or anything you want to remember (for example, if the child was sick or if there was a visitor in the classroom). This column can help you put the data into context later.

For behaviors that are more frequent, you can use the basic frequency chart like on page 99, or you can use the chart found in appendix O, which provides more specific information about when the behaviors occurred. The chart below shows the frequency data for Sahana's attention-seeking behaviors.

FREQUENCY CHART

Child: Sahana
Date: March 13

TIME PERIOD	FREQUENCY OF BEHAVIORS	NOTES
8:00–9:00	3	
9:00–10:00	2	
10:00–11:00	5	This was free play time. During a large portion of this time period, Ms. Santos was completing paperwork at her desk.
11:00–12:00	1	Sahana was sitting next to Ms. Santos during group activities, so it is possible that she was already getting enough attention and did not need to engage in attention-seeking behaviors.
12:00–1:00	4	Lunchtime and classroom cleanup

TIME PERIOD	FREQUENCY OF BEHAVIORS	NOTES
1:00–2:00	0	Naptime: Sahana fell asleep at about 12:45 and woke up at 2:15.
2:00–3:00	2	
3:00–4:00	4	
4:00–5:00	3	Sahana's mom picked her up from school at 4:30.

As we can see from the chart, Sahana's attention-seeking behaviors are spread out throughout the day. There is not one time interval that seems to be more problematic for Sahana. This tells us that her behaviors are likely not triggered by a certain activity and are related to having a specific need met. You will also notice in the "Notes" column that Sahana was asleep for an entire time interval. Without that note, we could easily look at this form and think that she just had an awesome hour.

FOR BEHAVIORS THAT LAST A LONG TIME

Frequency counts work well for most challenging behaviors. However, for temper tantrums, I recommend that you also track the length of the tantrum. It is valuable to know not only whether the tantrums are less common but also whether they are becoming shorter in length. Both of these can be indications that the intervention is working. Appendix Q provides a Behavior Duration Chart that you can use for this purpose, and I provide a sample completed Behavior Duration Chart on page 102. You will notice that I used the same chart both before and after starting the intervention. This helps me easily see whether the intervention is making a difference in the duration of the temper tantrum. You will also notice that the duration of the tantrum is not really any different before and after starting the intervention. Based on the fact that this particular chart includes only a few days after starting the intervention, we can assume that the intervention has not yet had time to impact Joey's behavior.

DATE	TIME BEHAVIOR STRARTED	TIME BEHAVIOR ENDED	TOTAL TIME	NOTES
October 7	9:17 a.m.	9:31 a.m.	14 minutes	Wanted to eat a cookie from his lunchbox during snack. Mr. Marco told him that he would need to save the cookie for lunchtime.
October 7	2:49 p.m.	3:56 p.m.	67 minutes	Wanted the red tricycle on the playground, but Ralph was already using the tricycle. Tantrum started about 5 minutes after going to playground and ended when Mom came to pick him up from school. Mr. Marco tried to talk to him during tantrum, but Joey refused to respond.
October 10	11:25 a.m.	11:40 a.m.	15 minutes	Joey wanted the red car in the transportation center. Kamal already had the car and would not give it to Joey.
October 13	9:14 a.m.	9:32 a.m.	18 minutes	First day of intervention! Joey wanted to sit next to Sarah at the snack table, but Sarah told him that she did not want to sit by him.
October 14	12:07 p.m.	1:05 p.m.	58 minutes	Joey was upset that his mom forgot to pack a cookie in his lunchbox. The tantrum ended when he fell asleep at the table.

HOW TO KNOW IF THE INTERVENTION IS WORKING

As mentioned in the previous section, you will need to collect data after beginning intervention in the same manner as you did before implementing the change. This is a very important step for knowing whether the intervention is working. The reality is that our perceptions of behavior may not always be accurate. The incidence of a particular behavior may start to slow down, but even occasional challenges may lead us to believe that the intervention is not working. Or our desire to find an effective intervention may convince us that an intervention is working when in reality it is not. Continuing to take data will show you the true picture of what is happening in your classroom. Plus, when the data shows that the intervention is working, you can use this information to share the success with the parents and your preschool director.

As you are taking data, please do not be discouraged if you do not see change for a few days. It is also possible that the behavior will get much worse before it gets better. Be patient. Give the intervention time to work before throwing it out the window. Just like you would not set a goal of running a marathon and then quit when you were unable to run the whole distance after just a week of training, you should not stop an intervention simply because there are not immediate results. I recommend consistently implementing the intervention and taking good data for at least two weeks before making any decisions. If you have not seen any improvement in the behavior by then, you should consider a different intervention. However, it is important to realize that two weeks is enough time to see improvement but not enough time for the behavior to completely disappear. That may take weeks or even months. Behavior change takes time, but remember that it is worth it. You are teaching skills that will help the child their entire life. Isn't that super awesome to think about? You are a life changer!

MOVING FORWARD

Now that you understand a little about how to implement interventions, head over to chapter 10 to learn about the specific interventions I recommend. I will be there waiting for you.

CHAPTER 10

Tier 2 Interventions in the Preschool Classroom

Mr. Hiroshi has worked hard this year to establish a solid Tier 1 PBIS program. As he reflects on this school year versus last year, he is amazed at how much less time he spends managing challenging behaviors. He feels like the children are learning so much more and he is less stressed at the end of each day. However, Mr. Hiroshi knows that Tier 1 is not enough to manage all of the behaviors in his classroom. He has three children in his morning class and two in the afternoon who are frequently in trouble with him and the floater who comes in during his lunch break. Mr. Hiroshi wants to do more to help these children be successful. He has determined that the functions of their behaviors are to gain his attention and to avoid challenging work.

Like Mr. Hiroshi, if you have come to this point in the book and have been implementing PBIS as intended along the way, you have likely noticed fewer challenging behaviors in your classroom. But the awesome systems you have put into place are not enough. A few children in your classroom still need more support. These children are going to need small group and individualized interventions in Tiers 2 and 3 of PBIS.

Before we move on to discuss Tier 2, though, I want to provide you with a few words of encouragement. You are becoming a PBIS rock star! You have implemented a solid Tier 1 and have identified the children who need extra support. You have conducted a behavior assessment and created behavior plans. Now you are ready to implement Tier 2 interventions. I am so proud of you and your dedication to the success of young children!

WHAT IS TIER 2?

It has likely been a while since you started reading this book, so I want to quickly remind you about the three tiers of PBIS. As we talked about in chapter 2, PBIS includes three tiers. The first tier is prevention efforts that are provided to all children. Tier 1 on its own should prevent about 85 percent of behavior challenges. For the 15 percent of children who need more than Tier 1 prevention, like those mentioned in Mr. Hiroshi's class at the beginning of the chapter, we provide small-group interventions at Tier 2 and individualized interventions at Tier 3. When you decide that a child needs more than Tier 1, you first try small-group interventions at Tier 2. If you try those interventions for a few weeks and they still are not enough, then you can move to individualized interventions at Tier 3. Ultimately, our goal is for children to be successful with the least amount of support. As you move into higher tiers, you are providing more support, so before you make the decision to do this, you need to see whether the child can meet behavior expectations without high levels of support.

At this point, it is also important to remind you that no child will have perfect behavior all of the time. Nobody is perfect. I know that I sometimes make mistakes or the wrong choices, and I'm sure that you do too. Remember that we should never expect more out of children than we expect out of ourselves, so we need to be willing to forgive occasional mistakes or misbehavior. However, when the behavior is frequent or severe, you should consider Tier 2 interventions. The rest of this chapter provides small-scale and easy-to-implement interventions that are effective for changing behaviors for groups of children or individual children. These interventions are considered Tier 2 because they are simple, do not generally need to be planned in advance, and can be implemented for any child when needed.

As you prepare to implement Tier 2 and use interventions to reduce or eliminate challenging behaviors, there is one thing that you should know: behavior often gets much worse before it gets better! It would be awesome if we started an intervention and behaviors changed immediately, but in many cases that is not the reality. Remember that the particular behavior has filled a certain function for a long time, and it will be hard for a child to stop getting his needs met through that behavior. When the behavior is no longer working for the child, they may try harder (use the same behavior more intensely) in the hopes that it will still work. As an example, if Asa always got your attention by screaming across the classroom and you suddenly start expecting her to raise her hand, she may start yelling louder and maybe even stomping her feet to get you to pay attention. Please know that this is normal, and when this happens, it is a sign that you are doing a great job of implementing your behavior plan. Be patient with your intervention; it will take time to work.

Okay, now let's chat about some good Tier 2 interventions. The specific interventions I recommend in Tier 2 are the following:

- removal of the problem-causing item

- time-out from the activity

- redirection/distraction

- nonverbal cues

- visual reminders and cues

- providing choice

- behavior-specific praise

- pre-correction statements

REMOVAL OF THE PROBLEM-CAUSING ITEM

As you take data on behavior challenges, you might notice that there is one toy or area of the room that is frequently a factor in misbehavior. Years ago, I was talking to a teacher about behavior, and she mentioned that her children always seemed so much more aggressive and got into a lot more trouble for behavior in the springtime, particularly around April. She assumed it had to do with coming back from spring break and being excited for summer. However, as I talked to the teacher some more, I realized that the behavior may have had more to do with her spring curriculum. To celebrate the beginning of baseball season, she always created a baseball center in her classroom during April. The center included all of the equipment needed to play baseball—balls, gloves, bases, and a few plastic bats. It was a fabulous real-world center that helped the children make connections with what was happening in their community, but I bet you are shaking your head right now because you know what I am about to say next. Yes, the children used the bats to hit one another and to knock toys down off of shelves. They just could not help themselves! I suggested to the teacher that she choose a different springtime center instead (possibly gardening but without shovels). She was hesitant because she really loved the baseball center, but she tried it. And, guess what? The April behavior challenges were no longer an issue. When she looked at behavior data for that year, April looked like every other month.

At this point, you might be thinking, "Well, duh! Who gives preschoolers bats and expects them not to hit one another?" But, in reality, all of us create components of our curriculum that may be the cause of problems. Wooden blocks are fun for building but are also used for hitting others. The pink sparkly ball is so pretty and everyone wants it, so there is a fight over the ball on the playground every day. Having paint available at all times allows for a lot of creativity, but it also leads to the classroom walls being painted on occasion. The specific problem-causing toy in your classroom may be different from these examples, but I would bet that if you think about it for a few minutes, you can identify at least one toy or center in your classroom that is regularly involved in children's misbehavior. So my questions to you are "Why is that toy still in your classroom? What benefit does it provide?"

It is okay to put limits on toys. The reality is that certain toys trigger misbehavior for some children. This might be true for just one child in your classroom or for several. But even if a certain toy causes problems for just one child, their behavior will likely cause trouble for other children. So put the toy in a closet for a few weeks or months. Or put limits on when the toy can be used. There may be toys that can be used only with teacher supervision or only when a child is playing alone—this is fine.

Earlier in this section, I mentioned wooden blocks. We all know that blocks are fabulous for learning to design and create, but they are also used as weapons by some children. However, for NAEYC-accredited preschools, blocks are also required as part of the physical environment in the classroom. Even if they are not required, we know that blocks help increase both science and math skills, so they are a valuable learning material in all preschool classrooms. I highly recommend that you purchase alternatives to the wooden blocks (though I still suggest owning wooden blocks and using them as appropriate). Foam and cardboard blocks make wonderful building tools, and it hurts a lot less to be hit with foam than with wood!

Take a few minutes right now and write down on a sticky note one toy that you might consider a problem-causing item in your classroom. Then come up with a plan for how to remove it, either permanently or by limiting its use.

TIME-OUT FROM THE ACTIVITY

On some days, we find that a certain activity or person is the primary trigger for a child's behavior. In those cases, the child may need a time-out from the activity. It is important to realize that this is not a traditional time-out. The child will not be removed from the rest of the class and will not be stuck in a corner somewhere. Instead, they will simply lose the privilege to play with a specific toy or interact with a certain person for a short stretch of time (usually about five minutes).

At this point, you are likely trying to think of a specific instance where you might use this Tier 2 intervention. Here are two examples from my teaching experience. Juanita loved to play with the shopping cart and always made a beeline for the dramatic play center during free play time just so she could be the first person to get the shopping cart. One day she got the cart and immediately began driving it into the wall. *Boom, boom, boom*. I quickly went over and reminded Juanita of the expectations regarding playing with the cart. Then I demonstrated for her how we play with a shopping cart (put food inside, have a baby doll sit in the front, and gently push it around the classroom, being careful not to hit anything or anyone). After that, I left her to play. For a few minutes, she pushed the cart and weaved in and out of the centers. But, I soon heard *boom, boom, boom* again as she slammed the shopping cart into the wall over and over. At this point, I went over and said, "Juanita, I am so sad to see that you are not making good choices with the shopping cart. Just a few minutes ago, I reminded you of how to use it correctly, and you chose not to follow my instructions. So you are going to lose the shopping cart for five minutes. During this time, you can go play with anything else in our classroom. When the time is up, you may try again to show me that you know how to use a shopping cart correctly." Then, I put the shopping cart in the hallway and set a timer for five minutes. After five minutes, I got the cart and gave it back to Juanita. At this point, she used it correctly and was able to use it for the rest of free play time. However, if she had chosen to use it for hitting the wall again, I would have taken it away for another five minutes. After the third time, Juanita would have lost it for the rest of the day and we would have started anew the next day.

I had another child in my classroom who loved my attention, and he wanted me to talk to him and play with him all day long. I imagine that you have a child just like this in your classroom. He may stand next to you for most of the day, scream your name across the room, or pull on you to get you to pay attention. Greyson was a sweet little boy, but his need for constant attention was annoying sometimes and often made it hard for me to help the other children in the classroom. To get me to pay attention, Greyson would first yell my name. If I did not respond quickly, he would come over to me and hit me until I paid attention to him. It is important to remember that Greyson was not trying to be mean and he was not trying to hurt me. He simply did not have the social skills or understanding to get my attention in any other way. However, his behavior was still unacceptable and needed to be addressed immediately. Because the function of Greyson's behavior was attention (for a reminder about the functions of behavior, look back at chapter 8), my attention could not be the result of his behavior. So, when Greyson hit me, he received a time-out from Mrs. L. As soon as he hit me, I would look at him and say, "Greyson, you hit me. That hurts my body, and I do not like it. Because you are not being kind to me, I am going to walk away for five minutes." This time-out from me meant that he could play with any other child or adult, but for five minutes he could not play with me or interact with me in any way. After the five-minute period, he could try again. On some days, he would just need one time-out from me, and on other days, he needed several. But as the year went on, we needed to use this strategy less and less.

Time-outs from activities are guided by very specific rules. The guidelines and steps are listed in appendix R. I highly recommend that you make a copy of the appendix and post it where you and every other adult who works in your classroom can see it. As with every other behavior management tool, it is important to do time-outs correctly.

REDIRECTION/DISTRACTION

The next Tier 2 intervention is one that I suspect you are already using on a regular basis. For many young children, distraction or redirection is an effective way to address challenging behaviors. When children are struggling, stopping the behavior can sometimes be as simple as getting their attention focused on something different. This is more effective with younger children, but it does sometimes work to change behavior for children of any age.

To redirect a child (or multiple children), you simply say something or offer something that will distract them, thus making the behavior stop. If Zahra is screaming because someone else has the baby stroller and she has to wait for a turn, I might walk over to her and say, "Zahra, did I tell you what my dog Jack did this weekend? It was so funny! Do you want to hear my story?" Or, if Jin and Sam are fighting over the blue ball on the playground, I can offer them another blue ball or a red ball. The use of redirection is meant to be fast, simple, and not time-consuming on your part.

When using redirection, it is important that you ensure that the redirection itself does not become a reward. If Raúl's favorite toy is the green car and you let him play with the green car only when you are redirecting him from an unacceptable behavior, he will quickly figure this out, and the instances of behavior problems will increase instead of decrease. Because of this, I highly recommend that you vary the objects you offer when you are redirecting a child and do not use their most preferred toys for this purpose.

NONVERBAL CUES

In recent years, there has been a lot of discussion about nonverbal communication, and I am sure that you are familiar with the many ways your body language can say more than your actual words. Nonverbal cues and reminders can be a great tool for providing children with a simple reminder of the behavior expectations in your classroom or to indicate that their current behavior is not acceptable. In addition, nonverbal cues can be used from across the classroom without disrupting the learning of other children (as opposed to yelling at Kamal, which makes all the children stop what they are doing and look at either you or Kamal). When choosing a nonverbal cue, I recommend considering the cultural implications of the particular cue, because the meaning of some nonverbal communication may differ for various cultures; for example, as mentioned previously, the thumbs-up sign can be considered vulgar. Examples of effective nonverbal cues for challenging behaviors in the preschool classroom include the following:

- holding up your hand like a stop sign

- shaking your head "no"

- pointing to something you need/want the child to do (point to the sink after Billy finishes using the restroom to remind him to wash his hands)

- putting your finger to your lips to indicate children need to be quiet

- puting your hands over your ears to indicate that the classroom is too loud

- raising your eyebrows to indicate that the child should stop the behavior

- making eye contact (note: the message indicated by eye contact differs greatly by culture, so use this nonverbal cue with caution)

- touching the child's arm to indicate they should stop doing something

- pointing to the Classroom Expectations poster

VISUAL REMINDERS AND CUES

Just like adults, children sometimes forget what is expected of them. They have a lot to remember, and sometimes they simply cannot remember everything. Imagine if I asked you to read this entire book in one day and begin implementing PBIS as I have explained it, but you could not refer back to the book or your notes. You would tell me that I am crazy and that it is impossible to do this. Well, many times the children in our classrooms feel the same way. We are asking them to remember a lot of things, and their brains simply cannot do it. They are doing their best, but they are frankly overwhelmed and they need our help to process all of the information we are giving them.

We can help young children remember better in a variety of ways, and one of my favorites is the use of visual supports. Many different types of visual cues exist that we can use, but I highly recommend you start with classroom schedules and task analysis. Each of these serves a different purpose and will help children be more successful.

Classroom schedules help children understand the plan for the day. For some young children, uncertainty about what is going to happen can be scary, and that fear may lead to inappropriate behaviors. To support these children, you can create a very simple daily schedule for your classroom. It does not need to be fancy. The best way to do this is to choose images that represent activities in your day (for example, I like to use a paintbrush to indicate art time). You can also use photographs of objects and children in your classroom. Print the images, laminate them, and put them in the correct order every day. During morning circle time (or your first morning activity), go over the schedule with the class. Then post the schedule in a location that all children can easily access in case they need a reminder about what is happening in the classroom that day.

The second type of visual cue that supports children's behavior is a task analysis. While the term *task analysis* sounds fancy, it is simply a list of steps for completing the task. For example, when I was a teacher, I noticed that children often skipped steps when washing their hands. So I created a simple task analysis with pictures for each step—turn on water, put hands under water, put soap on hands, rub hands together, put hands under water again, get paper towel, dry hands, turn off water with paper towel, throw away paper towel. I taught the children the steps for washing their hands, using the task analysis as a guide. Finally, I posted one copy of the task analysis above each sink in the restroom and one above the classroom sink. Whenever I noticed children skipping steps in washing their hands at our classroom sink, I could easily walk over and use the nonverbal cue of pointing to remind them of the missed step.

PROVIDING CHOICE

I don't know about you, but I really like to have some control over my life. I do not want someone else to make every decision for me. Children of all ages share this desire, and some children will have behavior challenges simply because they want more control over their lives. To prevent behaviors caused by a need for control (and to support children's autonomy), I recommend providing choices throughout the day. You can give children a choice in many ways while still ensuring that you are able to meet the daily learning outcomes. Think about your ultimate goal and then consider the various ways that children can achieve that goal. Here are a few ideas for providing choice in your preschool or kindergarten classroom. You will notice that each of these choices does not change the ultimate learning goal but does give the child some amount of control during the activity:

- crayon or marker for the art project

- stand or sit during circle time

- eat the banana or pancake first at breakfast

- take off coat independently or have teacher help to take off coat

- use the restroom before or after snack

- liquid soap or bar soap for washing hands

BEHAVIOR-SPECIFIC PRAISE

Another simple intervention that can be used for one child, a group of children, or the entire class is behavior-specific praise. Children (and adults) like to know that our efforts have been noticed and were appreciated. When using praise, being specific is critical. Tell the children exactly what they did well. You should specifically mention the behavior, mention the name of the child(ren), and ensure that your praise sounds positive. You should try to praise children as soon as possible after they engage in the desired behavior. If you wait very long (even more than a minute or two), the praise will have less of an impact, as the child may have forgotten what happened and has likely moved on to something else. Praise is an especially good intervention for children who are seeking teacher attention, such as the three students in Mr. Hiroshi's classroom.

In addition to being specific with your praise, it is also important that you do not overuse praise—do not praise every single thing that a child does. If you overpraise, children will stop listening and start to believe that you do not really mean it. But at the same time, you should use praise often enough so that children know when they are doing well. Think about expectations that are hard for the child, and praise them for the effort and willingness to do the task. Praise children for meeting your behavior expectations, especially when they do not always do so. The chart below provides a list of behavior-specific praise statements you can start using in your own classroom today; the underlined words can be replaced with the specific action you want to praise or the name of the child. The chart can also be found in appendix S. I recommend that you copy this and post it in your classroom.

EXAMPLES OF BEHAVIOR-SPECIFIC PRAISE FOR YOUNG CHILDREN

Angela, I like that you are sitting on your spot.

Baya, you are doing a great job of sharing the baby doll.

Chan, thank you for cleaning up the toys.

Danita, thumbs-up for staying in circle time today!

Ellie, high five for writing your letters. I know that it is hard for you.

Francesco, I am proud of you for flushing the toilet without a reminder.

Gabriela, great job of using your inside voice while you play monsters.

Henrik, fantastic work of putting your backpack in your cubby this morning.

Isaiah, excellent work of using your words when José had the car you wanted.

PRE-CORRECTION STATEMENTS

The final intervention in this chapter is one of my very favorites. This intervention is called pre-correction statements, which is just a fancy way of saying thank you to someone for doing something even before they do it. By saying thank you, we remind children to complete a particular action, and we provide them with praise for doing it before they do it. In the preceding section, we talked about the power of praise. It is a strong motivator for many children. When you praise a child for doing something before they do it, there is a huge likelihood that they will actually follow through and do it.

Let me give you a few examples. I want the children in my classroom to throw away their trash after snacktime. Goldfish bags and granola bar wrappers on the table drive me crazy! As we near the end of snacktime, I say, "Thank you so much for throwing away your trash before you go play in centers." And do you know what happens when they finish eating? They throw away their trash! It is the coolest thing. In addition to disliking trash on the table, unwashed hands also stress me out (little kids can be so germy). When a child asks to use the restroom, I say something like, "Of course you may go, and thank you for flushing the toilet and washing your hands when you are done." I bet you can guess what happens almost every time. Pre-correction statements can feel like magic.

As a side note, pre-correction is magic for adults too. I certainly hope that my husband is not reading this chapter (and, if you are—Mark, skip to chapter 11). There are certain household chores that I truly dislike. One of those is taking the trash dumpsters to the curb on trash day. I don't know why, but I really hate it. So, on Monday mornings (when I remember), I tell Mark to have a great day at work, and then I tell him I love him and thank him for taking out the trash. And guess what happens? It's magic, y'all!

MOVING FORWARD

Wow! We have made it through ten chapters now. You have only two more chapters before you are done. I am having so much fun talking about PBIS with you, and I love thinking about the successes you are now having in your classrooms (and I would love for you to send me an email or a tweet to share your story!).

CHAPTER 11

Tier 3 Interventions in the Preschool Classroom

Mrs. Perez has been using PBIS since the school year started. It was hard at first, but now that the school year is about halfway over, she is feeling confident in her behavior management skills and has seen significantly fewer problems in her classroom than in previous years. She has noticed that the children in this year's class seem to be scoring higher on her school's academic assessments than children from previous years. Mrs. Perez believes that this is due to the fact that PBIS has allowed her to spend less time managing behavior and more time teaching. Despite the success she is seeing, Mrs. Perez still has one child about whom she is concerned. Almost daily, Timmy hits or kicks someone else in the classroom, most often Mrs. Perez or other teachers. Mrs. Perez has heard from Timmy's previous teacher that he used to hit and kick five to ten times each day, so this year is an improvement. However, it is still not good enough, and Mrs. Perez is looking for support to help Timmy succeed.

Like Mrs. Perez, you have probably noticed that the undesirable behaviors in your classroom have decreased, but they have not all disappeared. I bet there are one or even two children in your classroom who are not quite meeting your behavior expectations. If you remember when we first talked about the PBIS pyramid (way back in chapter 2), I explained that a few children will be at the top of the pyramid and need individualized interventions. For these children, it is especially important that you look at the behavior assessment you conducted (the information on that process is located in chapter 8). Based on the fact that Tier 2 interventions were not sufficient for changing the behavior, you should consider adapting the behavior plan you have created (look at chapter 9 for the information on that process). In fact, I recommend that you take more data to ensure that you fully understand that function(s) of the child's behavior so that you can use interventions that are directly related to that function. Once you have done this, you need to choose one (or more) interventions that you believe will change the child's behavior. The interventions at Tier 3 will be more time-consuming and require significantly more effort than the interventions you used in Tier 2. However, if you find the right intervention, you will save time in the long run because you will be managing fewer behaviors in your classroom.

PLANNED IGNORING OF BEHAVIOR

The first Tier 3 intervention is one that I personally do not recommend. However, I have found that this particular intervention is frequently recommended by behavior "experts" and other well-meaning folks, so I want to present it and ensure that you know how to do it properly if you so choose. This intervention is **planned** ignoring of **behavior**. You will notice that I have bolded the words *planned* and *behavior*. If you try this intervention (and remember that I do not recommend you doing so), it is very important that you remember that all ignoring must be intentional and that you are supposed to ignore only the behavior, not the child. Planned ignoring works only when the function of the child's behavior is adult attention. This strategy won't work if the function is attention from other children, because it is unlikely that you will be able to get the other children to ignore their classmate.

Here is how this intervention works. When the child engages in the problem behavior, you must completely ignore it. You cannot respond in any way, either verbally or nonverbally. You cannot say, "Stop," or raise your eyebrows. You must continue teaching and act like everything is normal. In addition, you must still speak to the child and show high levels of respect to him without indicating that you are noticing his behavior. There must be zero indications that you are aware of the behavior the child is exhibiting.

Now that you know how to use the strategy of planned ignoring of behavior, here is why I do not recommend it. I mentioned in the last chapter that behaviors sometimes get worse before they get better. This is often especially true of attention-seeking behaviors. The child has learned that the behavior works for getting attention. When the behavior no longer results in adult attention, the child will try harder and harder. And you must ignore the behavior no matter how bad it gets. For example, if Liam frequently yelled my name from across the room when he wanted my attention and I suddenly started ignoring the yelling, he would first try yelling louder. When that did not work, he might try coming closer to me and yelling. And when that did not work, I might quickly find Liam screaming in my ear to get my attention. If I respond even once (and, let's be honest, it is very hard not to respond when someone screams in my ear), Liam will quickly learn that yelling my name still meets the function of getting my attention but only in its most extreme form, so he will start yelling in my ear every single time he wants me to pay attention to him. Or if Mrs. Perez began ignoring Timmy's hitting and kicking, he would try hurting others more until he got a response. The reason I do not recommend ignoring behavior is that it is often too hard to ignore the behavior once it becomes extreme, and this intervention will work only if you and all other adults in the classroom are 100 percent committed and do not *ever* respond to the behavior.

Now that I have explained to you how to use the one Tier 3 intervention that I recommend avoiding, here are my recommendations for evidence-based strategies for young children who need additional behavior support:

- teaching new skills

- teaching replacement behaviors

- structured breaks

- individualized visual cues

- rewards

- behavior contracts

- sensory tools

TEACHING NEW SKILLS

In some cases, especially for young children, behavior problems can be a sign that the child does not currently possess the necessary skills to complete what you expect. This does not mean that they cannot do what you want. It simply means that you will need to teach them. Remember that many of the expectations we have for young children in our classrooms are different from the expectations in their homes or in other settings. It is unlikely that they are expected to walk in a line or sit criss-cross applesauce at home. And many young children live with no other children in their homes, so the concept of sharing, especially sharing preferred toys or the attention of their favorite people, is a skill they have not had much opportunity to master. When a child has a skill deficit, it may appear to us that they are misbehaving when, in reality, they simply do not understand the expectations.

When you are considering the possibility that a child may need instruction to gain a new skill, be sure that you determine the developmental appropriateness of that skill. It would be unfair to the child (and a waste of your time) to try teaching a skill that is not developmentally appropriate or a skill for which the child does not have the necessary prerequisite skills.

Once you are sure that the behavior expectation is developmentally appropriate, begin planning how to teach the skill to the child. Think way back to chapter 6 when we talked about the importance of teaching classroom expectations through the use of a structured lesson plan. To teach a new skill, you will need to do the same thing. I really love education professor Madeline Hunter's lesson-plan format and suggest that you include the components she recommends:

1. Activation of background knowledge

2. Anticipatory set

3. Statement of the objective

4. Input/modeling

5. A check for understanding

6. Guided practice

7. Independent practice

In most cases, you will need to provide this explicit instruction on the desired skill to only one child, so you can easily do that with one-on-one lessons that you teach during free play time or while you have another adult lead the large-group instruction for your class. However, if more than one child is having a hard time with the skill or you think the entire class could use a refresher in what is expected, circle time and other group instructional times are good places to teach new skills or review previously learned skills.

TEACHING REPLACEMENT BEHAVIORS

Just as some children do not have the skills to complete the expected behavior, other children have the skills but may not know how to use them at the right time, leading to inappropriate behavior. In the preceding chapter, I talked about Greyson, who would first yell from across the room if he wanted my attention and then, if I did not respond, would often kick me to get my attention. I don't like it when children yell at me or kick me to get my attention, so I wanted to help Greyson change his behavior as quickly as possible. To do that, I needed to teach him a replacement behavior. A replacement behavior is a socially appropriate behavior that meets the same function as the behavior we want to eliminate. So, for Greyson, I needed to teach him a different way to get my attention. Teaching Greyson a replacement behavior can be done using the same Madeline Hunter steps we talked about but with one change. After teaching the skill, you will need to practice, practice, practice with the child. You should practice as many times as possible each day, but make sure that you are practicing when the child is calm and does not yet need to use the skill. Please do not try to have the child practice "in the moment"—without a lot of practice and role play, the child will fail.

Before you begin this process of teaching a replacement behavior, you should complete appendix T to help you think through the current challenging behavior, what you would like the child to do instead, and how you can help the child learn the replacement skill. Keep in mind that this form is just for you, not for colleagues or parents, so you can just jot down notes and keywords, and you do not need to use complete sentences and explain everything. I have completed appendix T for Greyson to show you how you might fill this out. Like all of the other forms in this book, I highly recommend that you take time completing it and are as thorough as possible, as better planning will lead to better results. Being flexible in your planning is also critical, as what you outline in appendix T may have to be adjusted to meet the child's responses to your instruction or changing needs of the classroom.

1. Describe the challenging behavior.

> When Greyson wants my attention, he yells my name across the room. If he tries this five or six times (based on the observational data I took today) and I do not respond, he will walk over to me and begin hitting or kicking me. He keeps hitting or kicking until I pay attention to him.

2. Why is this behavior a problem?

> Hitting and kicking hurt! I have bruises on my arms and legs, and I do not like it! In addition, if the behavior continues in kindergarten, Greyson will be suspended from school and may face social consequences from classmates.

3. What is usually the result (consequence: good or bad) of the behavior?

> When Greyson hits or kicks me, he receives a time-out from me. However, the process of getting him to that time-out requires my attention. So he is still ultimately getting my attention, at least for a few minutes.

4. What would I like the child to do instead (that still meets the same function)?

> I would like Greyson to raise his hand and wait for me to come to him or for Greyson to walk over to me and wait patiently until I acknowledge him.

5. Why will my desired replacement behavior work better?

> Greyson will get more of my attention, and that attention will be positive. But it will take longer to get my attention, so it might feel to Greyson as though the replacement behaviors are not working as well.

6. What are the specific steps of the replacement behavior?

> *Steps for Raising Hand*
> 1. Sit/stay where he is.
> 2. Keep his mouth closed.
> 3. Raise his hand.
> 4. Wait silently.
> 5. Upon acknowledgment, ask for my attention.
> 6. Receive attention.
>
> *Steps for Waiting Next to Me*
> 1. Silently walk from where he is over to me.
> 2. Stand about one foot away from me.
> 3. Silently stand and wait to be acknowledged.
> 4. Once acknowledged, tell me what he wants/needs.

7. What challenges do I foresee in teaching the replacement behavior?

- Greyson has used the strategies of screaming and hitting/kicking for a long time. He may be resistant to trying something new.
- Because he will be silent, there is a good chance that I may not know immediately that Greyson wants attention. If my response is delayed, he may think this replacement behavior does not work.
- There are ten other children in the classroom who also need my attention—I cannot give them all attention at once!

8. What is my plan for teaching the replacement behavior?

- Use one-on-one lessons during free play time—initially write three lesson plans and rotate them.
- Start with ten-minute lessons during morning free play, after-lunch playground time, and afternoon free play.
- Role-play in person and with puppets/stuffed animals.
- Stay within five feet of Greyson during all free play times to ensure that I can see him raise his hand or that he can quickly stand next to me.
- Praise for every time Greyson attempts to get my attention appropriately, even when he does not succeed.
- Conversation with Greyson's mom tomorrow morning to explain the problem, discuss my teaching plan, and request her thoughts.

When Greyson was in my class, I needed to help him learn how to get my attention in an effective but acceptable way. My ultimate goal was for Greyson to raise his hand and wait for me to come to him or for Greyson to walk over to me and wait patiently until I acknowledged him. However, it was unrealistic to jump from his yelling/hitting behavior to that. So, I had to scaffold his learning and slowly teach him how to use these more acceptable ways of getting my attention. My plan, as outlined in Step 8, took several weeks to implement. At first Greyson attempted the replacement behaviors only once or twice a day and gave up if I did not notice him and respond within a minute. As time went on and he learned that I would respond, he was willing to wait longer and longer until eventually he would wait up to five minutes. It took considerable time, but the end result was worth it. And Greyson had a new skill that he could take with him for success in his next classroom.

STRUCTURED BREAKS

Staying on task and focusing on learning can prove challenging for many young children. School is hard work. Just like any hard work, to have success, you may require occasional breaks to rejuvenate. Even as a teacher of adults, I look forward to a few minutes of quiet during lunchtime, and I distinctly remember thinking that my two-minute restroom breaks were necessary for my sanity when I was a preschool teacher. Like us, children need breaks sometimes too. Some children will have a hard time controlling their behavior when they do not get enough breaks. For these children, I highly recommend scheduling breaks into their day.

When a child needs regular breaks, scheduling specific times throughout the day for those breaks can be helpful. The frequency and length of those breaks will depend on the specific needs of the child. Some children will need a break after every single activity, while others may just need one break midmorning and another midafternoon. For some children, one minute of closing their eyes while lying on the beanbag will be sufficient rest, and for others, ten minutes of jumping on a trampoline may be required. As you plan breaks, be flexible and willing to try a variety of setups to best accommodate the needs of the child. I also recommend offering extra breaks (in addition to those that are scheduled) on days when the child is struggling more than usual.

INDIVIDUALIZED VISUAL CUES

In the preceding chapter, we talked about using visual cues, such as visual schedules and task analysis. While the visual cues for the entire class can support most students, you may have one or two children who will benefit from having their own individualized visual cues. Some children will need their own copy of a visual schedule to keep with them all day. You can make a simple individualized schedule by putting the pictures in a file folder—these folders are the perfect size for a young child to carry, and they come in fun colors and designs to keep the child excited and motivated.

You may also need to create a simple task analysis for a child. For Greyson the replacement behavior (walking to me and standing next to me to get my attention) involves several steps. If Greyson forgets even one of those steps, he will be unable to complete the desired behavior. I can create a basic visual task analysis of the steps to help him out. When I create these visual supports for an individual child, I prefer to use photos of the child completing each step. This increases motivation, reminds the child that they are capable of completing the task, and triggers the child's memory of completing the steps. Individual task analysis can be printed on a piece of paper that is taped to the child's work space or can be placed on the front or back of the file folder that includes the visual schedule. The important piece is to ensure that the child understands the steps and has the visual cue available as a support when it is needed (so don't leave the visual support for Greyson at the lunch table if he is likely to want teacher attention during centers).

When you first give the visual cue (either the schedule or the task analysis) to a child, you will want to explicitly teach them how to use it. I recommend modeling and role play. In addition, for the first few weeks (and possibly longer), you should remind them to use it at appropriate times.

REWARDS

When we ask children to follow our classroom expectations, they may find it very hard. Frankly, doing what is expected all of the time is *work*. And people deserve to get paid for their work. I don't know about you, but despite how much I love my job, I would not go to work every single day and be away from my children so much if I did not get paid. And I have the very best job in the entire world. However, there are days that I would prefer to stay in bed or curl up by the fire with a hot coffee and a good book. On those days, my paycheck (and the small personal rewards that my salary allows me to buy—caramel macchiatos and new shoes) are part of my motivation. I want to be paid for my work, and so do the children in your classroom. You do not need to write them a check or give them money in any way, but rewards for meeting behavior expectations can decrease challenging behaviors.

At times it can be beneficial to provide rewards for all children in your classroom when they meet behavior expectations (and doing so will enhance the solid Tier 1 you have designed). But you may have a child or two who will need the intervention of rewards on a regular basis. This intervention is best paired with instruction on the desired behavior while supporting the child's use of the new skill you are teaching them. Your goal is to slowly phase out the reward interventions as the child becomes more consistent with meeting the behavior expectations and learns to do so without the extra support. You do not need to worry that Johnny is going to be thirty years old and still want a stamp on his hand every single time that he uses his words. He will eventually learn to do what you want without payment, but the use of rewards is going to help him learn faster.

Before we move forward, I want to quickly address what I know some of you are thinking. No, I am not suggesting that we bribe children to behave. A bribe is provided before the "work" is completed with the hope that it will lead to a good result. A reward is payment after the "work" is done. Think of a bribe as an advance on the paycheck and a reward as payment that comes when you have completed the work. I do not advocate bribing children, but I do firmly believe that rewarding children is appropriate and often necessary.

To provide rewards in your classroom, there are a few steps to take. First, you need to determine what the child views as a reward. Not all children are motivated by stickers or attention from the teacher. One of the easiest ways to learn a child's reward preferences is to ask. They will tell you! Appendix U provides a reward menu. A reward menu is simply a list of potential rewards that you are willing to offer the child for meeting behavior expectations. You will notice that I left each line blank so that you can add rewards specific to your classroom. To use the reward menu, sit down with the child and read each item listed. Have them circle either the smiley face or the frown face to indicate if they would like the potential reward listed. Then they should choose their top five rewards from the list. Use those as your primary rewards when you first begin using a reward system. Here are some sample ideas of simple items that are often rewarding to young children:

- receiving stickers

- obtaining stamps (especially on hands or feet)

- getting a positive note sent home telling parents about good behavior

- choosing where to sit at circle time (or lunchtime or the next activity of the day)

- being the line leader (either all day or just for the next activity)

- receiving one-on-one time with the teacher (this can be very short; two to three minutes is often rewarding)

- having quiet time in the classroom library

- sitting at the teacher's desk/in the teacher's chair

- being the teacher's helper for the next activity

- drawing on the dry-erase board

- playing with a preferred toy for a few minutes

- selecting a prize from the treasure box

After you have worked with the child to identify the items that are rewarding, you will need to identify the criteria for receiving the reward. Will you provide a reward every single time the child shows the desired behavior? Will you provide the reward every third time they do what you want? Will you provide the reward on a random schedule? (For young children, I do not recommend the latter—they tend to do better when they know exactly what to expect.) The frequency with which you provide rewards should be determined by the needs of the child. Joey might need a small reward every few minutes, while Sahana might only need one reward per day. Just make sure that you communicate to the child when rewards will be given.

Over time, but not until the problem behavior has completely (or almost completely) disappeared, you will want to slowly phase out the rewards. If Joey was receiving a reward every five minutes, you might move that interval to a reward every eight minutes. Then, once he is successful for at least two to thee days with that, you could move it to every twelve minutes. If possible, slowly increase the time between rewards until you are no longer providing a reward at all. But remember that it is okay if you are never able to do that. It is completely normal and acceptable for some children to need rewards for good behavior for many years. If other children notice Joey receiving rewards, simply tell them that in your classroom, "every child gets what he or she needs to be successful. Right now, Joey needs stickers."

BEHAVIOR CONTRACTS

Whenever possible, you should involve the child in your behavior management plan. One way to do this for older children is the use of a behavior contract. Essentially, this contract is an agreement that you, the child, and other stakeholders (like parents or other teachers in the classroom) create together and all sign. The behavior contract is an agreement that the child will do his best to meet behavioral expectations and that the adults around him will do their best to support him. A reward and the criteria for gaining the reward can be built into the contract. The use of a behavior contract puts the primary responsibility for appropriate behavior on the child and is most often appropriate for older preschoolers, such as those nearing their fifth birthday or older. A behavior contract can be created in a variety of ways:

- Written text: To do this, you will need to write what the child and adults agree to do (a sample written behavior contract is provided). This is the most common form of behavior contract and is used for children through high school, but a written contract is challenging when the child is a nonreader.

- Pictures/images: This is similar to a written contract, but you will use photographs or clip art images to indicate what the child and adults are all agreeing to do. This form of behavior contract will require significant discussion among all parties to ensure that everyone has the same understanding of each image.

- Video: To create a video contract, the child will verbalize on video what he agrees to do, and adults will verbalize how they agree to support the child. This form of behavior contract is still experimental, but my suspicion is that it would likely work well for young children.

Once you have created the contract, it is important that you review it (by reading or viewing) with the child at least once per day. If you know there is a certain activity that is likely to lead to a behavior challenge, I recommend reviewing the behavior contract just before that activity. When the child or adult fails to do what they agreed, they are accountable to the others as outlined in the contract. This accountability can be very motivating for some children.

This contract was created by Sara and Mrs. Lohmann on March 15. We have both agreed to what is stated below.

Sara agrees to

- keep her hands off her classmates' bodies
- keep her teeth off her classmates' bodies
- use her words when she is upset

Mrs. Lohmann agrees to

- review this contract with Sara every morning during breakfast
- provide reminders to Sara when she believes Sara might be getting upset
- make sure Sara has her chewing necklace at all times
- use behavior-specific praise when she notices that Sara is making good choices
- call Sara's daddy and mommy at least once per week to tell them when Sara is making good choices
- give Sara a *PJ Masks* sticker at lunchtime if Sara made good choices all morning
- give Sara a Daniel Tiger sticker at the end of the day if Sara made good choices all afternoon

We both agree to this contract and will do our best to follow what we promised.

_____   _____
        Sara   *Mrs. Lohmann*

SENSORY TOOLS

In chapter 8, we talked about the functions of behavior. One less prevalent but not uncommon function (especially for younger children) is sensory stimulation. When this is the case, you can help children meet the same function through the use of sensory tools. There is no magic formula for determining which sensory tools will work for a child, so you may have to try several of these. Many children will need a variety of sensory tools. Please note that this list is meant to stimulate your thinking, but it is not an exhaustive list. The specific sensory tool that works for a child may or may not be on this list:

- Velcro under a chair (the child can reach under the chair and play with the Velcro while seated)

- bumpy seat cushion

- foam mat for sitting on the floor

- soft blanket

- stuffed animal

- fidget balls (but be careful because many children throw these at others)

- grips for pencils, crayons, markers, and paintbrushes

- playdough

- putty or moon dough

- teething necklace or other "chewlery"

- gum for chewing (I know that many teachers do not like gum in the class-room, but remember that gum is a better way to meet an oral stimulation need than biting classmates.)

- Breathing exercises (I like to teach children to close their eyes and pretend to blow air "just like the wind.")

MOVING FORWARD

I am sitting here at my computer, thinking about the successes you are in your class-room. We are just one chapter away from being completely done with this book. I have had a blast working with you and am hoping that you are now feeling more confident in your classroom management skills. Meet me in the conclusion (page 131) for a recap of what we have discussed in the past eleven chapters and a short discussion of where we go from here.

Conclusion

There is a lot of information out there about interventions and behavior management. Just a few moments online will give you a ton of ideas for how to "solve the behaviors in your classroom." But as you have seen in this book, the solution is not a cartoon-themed behavior clip chart or rainbow-colored behavior punch cards. Instead, effective classroom behavior management involves hard work on your part and the implementation of an evidence-based prevention and intervention framework such as PBIS.

As reminder, PBIS is a three-tiered model that provides both prevention and intervention supports for all children in the classroom. PBIS can be illustrated through a pyramid as shown here. Tier 1 provides supports for all children in the classroom. Tier 2 is designed to meet the needs of a small group of children who need extra supports in meeting the classroom behavior expectations, and Tier 3 provides individualized interventions for children with the most challenging behaviors.

Tier 3
Individualized
Interventions

Tier 2
Small-Group Interventions

Tier 1
Universal Prevention Strategies

At all levels of PBIS, it is critical that we show respect for each child, show respect for the cultures represented in the classroom, use evidence-based practices, and use action-research to guide all decisions we make. At the Tier 1 level, we collaborate with families, build relationships with children, teach our classroom expectations, and ensure that we are using appropriate instruction. In Tier 2 we implement simple interventions, such as removing the problem-causing item; taking a "time-out" from the activity; providing redirection or distraction, nonverbal cues, visual reminders and cues, or multiple choices; giving behavior-specific praise; or making pre-correction statements. When a child requires the intense supports provided in Tier 3, we may choose to use strategies such as teaching new skills or replacement behaviors or providing structured breaks, individualized visual cues, rewards, behavior contracts, and sensory tools.

As we close our time together, I want to leave you with a few reminders and some critical things to consider:

- The first step in changing children's behavior is changing our own behavior.

- Our own biases will impact the ways in which we respond to children and behaviors, so teachers must take time to be aware of, and address, their bias.

- Children (and adults) are not perfect, so some inappropriate behavior is normal.

- Consistency in implementation and supports is critical for the success of a PBIS framework.

- Behavior change takes time. It may take days or even weeks for your PBIS system to show results. While you wait, be patient. As the old saying goes, "Good things come to those who wait."

- There is no one-size-fits-all answer to behavior management. What works one school year may not work the next. What works for the teacher next door might not work for you. What works with your morning preschool classroom may fail with your afternoon students. The important thing is to keep trying until you find the right interventions for you and for your students.

- In *all* interactions with a child, we need to be respectful of the child. Even if Bobby bites, hits, and kicks and we dislike being around him, we must treat him with the utmost respect. He is a child and he is still learning. And you have the greatest job on earth because you get to guide his learning and help him grow.

While reading this book, you have gained new knowledge and skills about implementing the PBIS framework in your classroom and school. To support your continued learning and implementation, I have included suggested resources and websites in appendix V.

FAREWELL FOR NOW

Thank you for spending the past twelve chapters with me. I have had the loveliest time, and I am encouraged to know that our time together is not over. I know that you will tweet to me about your success or maybe find me to chat at the next NAEYC or DEC conference. So farewell for now. Keep working hard to implement PBIS. Never give up on yourself or on the children in your classroom.

Discussion Guide

If you are lucky enough to be reading this book with colleagues (or, even better, with all of the faculty at your school), you will want to work together to develop a common PBIS system. Using the same basic PBIS framework in all classrooms will help children adjust as they move from one classroom to another and will help classroom floaters and other adults to support the needs of children in all rooms better.

I highly recommend that program-wide teams who are all working to implement PBIS plan to do a group study and work through this book together over the course of a semester or even an entire school year. One strategy that might work well is for a school-wide or program-wide team (meaning all faculty, full-time and part-time) to complete the book study in the spring/summer and then begin implementing the Tier 1 framework in the fall.

This chapter provides a brief list of discussion questions for teams to use as they meet to discuss the book. In addition to the discussion questions, I highly recommend that teams work together to complete the activities in this book. And feel free to send me your burning questions via Twitter. I'm @MarlaLohmann.

CHAPTER 1 QUESTIONS

1. Why are you interested in PBIS? Why are you completing this book study?

2. How do you feel about the time commitment that this book study/ implementing PBIS will take? Are you willing to keep trying this for the entire school year? What strategies will you use to keep yourself motivated during implementation?

3. How do you currently think about behavior? How does your current thinking differ (or does it) from the idea that behavior is a skill to be taught?

4. At this time, what supports do you need to work through this book?

5. How do you currently feel about PBIS? What are your fears? What are your hopes? What are your frustrations? What other feelings is this initiative invoking?

6. What burning questions do you currently have about PBIS?

CHAPTER 2 QUESTIONS

1. What is your impression of the research supporting PBIS? How does this evidence support your desire to implement PBIS (or does it)?

2. What are you hoping to gain from PBIS implementation? If different book study members have different goals, talk about how all of those goals will/can be met.

3. How will you evaluate the progress toward your PBIS goals?

4. What are the top three current behavior challenges in your classroom or school? How do the behavior challenges compare from one classroom to the next? Are the behaviors school-wide similar or different?

5. How do you feel about data collection? What feelings does the word *data* invoke in you? If you feel fear or disdain, how will you overcome that fear to use data to support children's growth and development?

6. What communication systems is the school using to provide information to stakeholders? What other communication systems might be considered?

7. What resources are available for supporting PBIS in the school? Are there resources that teachers can share? How can school faculty support one another to increase available resources?

8. How do you currently feel about PBIS? What are your fears? What are your hopes? What are your frustrations? What other feelings is this initiative invoking?

9. What burning questions do you currently have about PBIS?

CHAPTER 3 QUESTIONS

1. What diversity exists in your school/classrooms? How does that diversity impact learning?

2. What biases have you identified in your own teaching? How are you addressing these biases?

3. In what specific ways are you showing respect for all children?

4. Brainstorm additional ways to ensure that all children feel respected and appreciated for who they are as individuals.

5. How are you currently celebrating the diverse cultures and beliefs represented in your school?

6. Brainstorm additional ways to ensure that all cultures are represented in the classroom (library books, materials, celebrations, and so on). Think about ways that teachers can support one another and share resources and responsibilities for making this a reality.

7. What do you know about evidence-based practices? How will you ensure that the teaching strategies you are using are evidence based?

8. What resources do you currently use to locate teaching ideas? How do you know that those resources include research-based strategies?

9. Why is it important to use evidence-based strategies in your classroom?

10. How do you currently feel about PBIS? What are your fears? What are your hopes? What are your frustrations? What other feelings is this initiative invoking?

11. What burning questions do you currently have about PBIS?

CHAPTER 4 QUESTIONS

1. How do you currently welcome families to the school before they actually arrive?

2. What else could you do to make families feel welcome from day one (or before)?

3. How do you currently communicate with families? Is that working? If not, what other communication systems might be worth trying?

4. What do you think about "homework calendars"? What challenges might "homework" present for the families in your school? Is this a viable idea for increasing home-school collaboration? Why or why not?

5. How would you describe your interactions with families? Are they positive or negative? Are you following the 4:1 rule?

6. How do you feel about inviting families to your classroom? What hopes or fears do you have about an open-door policy that allows people to walk into your classroom at any time?

7. What barriers do you currently see to partnering with the families in your school? What specific action steps can you take to overcome those barriers?

8. How do you currently feel about PBIS? What are your fears? What are your hopes? What are your frustrations? What other feelings is this initiative invoking?

9. What burning questions do you currently have about PBIS?

CHAPTER 5 QUESTIONS

1. How would you describe the relationships you currently have with the children in your classroom?

2. Are there some children with whom you connect more easily? If so, why do you think that is?

3. How do you currently welcome children to your classroom (both at the beginning of the school year and on a daily basis)?

4. How are you celebrating the uniqueness of each child?

5. Are you taking time to play with the children in your classroom every day? If not, what barriers are preventing this from happening?

6. What specific action steps will you take to ensure that you are building relationships with all children?

7. How do you currently feel about PBIS? What are your fears? What are your hopes? What are your frustrations? What other feelings is this initiative invoking?

8. What burning questions do you currently have about PBIS?

CHAPTER 6 QUESTIONS

1. What are your biggest pet peeves in the classroom? What child behaviors trigger you to become frustrated?

2. Describe the ideal preschool child. How do they act?

3. In the chapter, we discuss the need to tell children what you want them to do. Share an example of a time when you thought you told children to do something, but your message was unclear to them (think of the example of Miguel).

4. In this chapter, you were asked to complete appendix H and then determine your classroom expectations. I highly recommend that each teacher complete appendix H and then you work together to categorize what you want children to do and determine the classroom expectations. You will be amazed at the fabulous ideas you come up with as a team—have fun as you decide your rules and work on designing the instructional materials.

5. How do you currently feel about PBIS? What are your fears? What are your hopes? What are your frustrations? What other feelings is this initiative invoking?

6. What burning questions do you currently have about PBIS?

CHAPTER 7 QUESTIONS

1. How has the implementation of Tier 1 PBIS changed your classroom/school?

2. How do you currently reflect on your instruction? Based on your reflection, what changes have you made to your teaching in the past?

3. What are your impressions of the UDL framework? It is okay if the thought of discussing yet another initiative right now is just too much—you can ignore this for now, if needed.

4. How do you currently support learners who are achieving about "average"? What can you do differently?

5. How do you currently support learners who are achieving below "average"? What can you do differently?

6. How do you currently ensure that all children are engaged in the learning activity? What can you do differently?

7. How do you currently support wiggly children? What can you do differently?

8. How do you currently feel about PBIS? What are your fears? What are your hopes? What are your frustrations? What other feelings is this initiative invoking?

9. What burning questions do you currently have about PBIS?

CHAPTER 8 QUESTIONS

1. What questions do you have about the functions of behavior? Are there certain behaviors for which you cannot identify the function? If so, help one another figure them out.

2. What is the function of your behavior in PBIS implementation? Why are you working through this book and implementing PBIS?

3. Who are the children you believe need extra behavior support? Do others in the school agree with your assessment, based on concerns they have heard you mention in the past and their observations of your class (from the playground or walking by your classroom door)?

4. If you have completed A-B-C charts before this discussion, I recommend that you bring them to share. Having an outside set of eyes look at your data may bring some new insight.

5. How do you currently feel about data? Is it becoming your friend, if it wasn't already? Why or why not?

6. How do you currently feel about PBIS? What are your fears? What are your hopes? What are your frustrations? What other feelings is this initiative invoking?

7. What burning questions do you currently have about PBIS?

CHAPTER 9 QUESTIONS

1. What behavior interventions are you currently using in your classrooms? Are they working?

2. What data collection techniques are you using? Do you have any new ideas for how to collect data easily and without disrupting instruction?

3. How do you feel about the statement in the chapter about behavior change taking time? How can you ensure that you are being patient with the change?

4. How do you currently feel about PBIS? What are your fears? What are your hopes? What are your frustrations? What other feelings is this initiative invoking?

5. What burning questions do you currently have about PBIS?

CHAPTER 10 QUESTIONS

1. How do you believe PBIS Tier 1 is working? What is working well? Is there anything you would like to tweak at this point?

2. Which children do you believe need Tiers 2 and 3 supports?

3. Are you currently using any of the interventions mentioned in chapter 10? If so, how are they working?

4. What center, toy, or activity is often a problem-causing item for the children in your classroom? Can you remove that item? If not, what can you do to reduce the problems that occur because of that item?

5. How can you support one another in creating materials for implementing interventions? (For example, each person can share what they have created for visual cues.)

6. What choices are you providing to the children in your classrooms? In what other ways can you provide choice? Are there any activities that are nonnegotiable and do not provide any choice? If so, how can you spread those nonnegotiable activities throughout the day so that children have choices between these activities?

7. How are you currently praising children? Are you using behavior-specific praise or just general praise? Practice giving behavior-specific praise to the other members of the book study.

8. Think of ways you can use pre-correction statements to encourage appropriate behaviors.

9. How do you currently feel about PBIS? What are your fears? What are your hopes? What are your frustrations? What other feelings is this initiative invoking?

10. What burning questions do you currently have about PBIS?

CHAPTER 11 QUESTIONS

1. How is PBIS Tier 1 currently working? Do you believe that classroom behavior challenges have decreased? Does the data support your belief?

2. What Tier 3 interventions as listed in chapter 11 are you currently using? How are they working?

3. What new skills/replacement behaviors are you preparing to teach to one child (or a small group of children)? How will you teach those skills? What supports do you need to effectively teach them?

4. If there is a skill you are planning to teach, this is a great opportunity to get help from other book study members in task analyzing that skill.

5. How do you feel about providing rewards to children?

6. How do you like to reward yourself for your hard work?

7. How is your school rewarding itself for PBIS implementation? If you are not, should you be?

8. What sensory tools do you have in your school that can be used to support children with sensory needs? Where are those tools located, and how can you access them when needed?

9. How do you currently feel about PBIS? What are your fears? What are your hopes? What are your frustrations? What other feelings is this initiative invoking?

10. What burning questions do you currently have about PBIS?

CONCLUSION QUESTIONS

1. As we have now reached the end of the book, how do you currently feel about PBIS? What are your fears? What are your hopes? What are your frustrations? What other feelings is this initiative invoking?

2. What success have you experienced with PBIS?

3. What challenges have you experienced?

4. If you were to implement PBIS from the beginning again, what would you do differently?

5. Based on your experiences and your feelings at this point, will you continue with PBIS? Why or why not?

Appendixes

APPENDIX A: PBIS PLANNING QUESTIONNAIRE

1. Why do I want to implement PBIS?

2. What challenging behaviors exist in my classroom?

3. Are these behaviors a problem for all students or just a few?

4. Who are the most challenging students in my classroom?

5. Which adults work in my classroom?

6. What specific routines must I follow?

7. What is the classroom layout, and do I have the freedom to rearrange it?

8. What systems do I use to communicate with stakeholders about my classroom?

9. What are the learning goals that my students must achieve?

10. What resources do I have available for supporting me in implementing PBIS?

11. What challenges do I foresee in PBIS implementation?

12. What are my fears about attempting PBIS?

APPENDIX B: PRE-PBIS IMPLEMENTATION DATA COLLECTION CHART

Date:

TIME	CHILD	BEHAVIOR

Yelling	
Wiggling	
Running around classroom	
Biting	
Saying "no" to teacher directions	
Stealing toys	
Hitting	
Throwing trash from snack onto floor	
Not washing hands after using toilet	
Kicking	
Spitting at others	

From *Positive Behavior Interventions and Supports for Preschool and Kindergarten* by Marla J. Lohmann, © 2021.
Published by Redleaf Press, www.redleafpress.org. This page may be reproduced for individual or classroom use only.

What Is PBIS?

Who: All stakeholders in the school/classroom: this includes children, teachers, parents, administrators, custodians, cooks, etc.

What: Supporting the growth and development of young children by implementing evidence-based prevention and intervention strategies aimed at addressing socially inappropriate behaviors

When: Starting now and every single day from now on

Where: PBIS implementation occurs in the school but works best when the efforts are also supported through caregiver messages in the home.

Why: To provide young children the skills they need for lifelong success

APPENDIX D: SAMPLE LETTER TO PARENTS

Dear Parents,

I am excited to share with you a new program we will soon be starting in our classroom. As a lifelong learner, I am constantly searching for new ways to support the learning and development of the children in my classroom. Recently I learned about a system called Positive Behavior Interventions and Supports, or PBIS. PBIS is a framework designed to support the social and emotional learning of children through direct teaching of behavioral expectations. The use of PBIS is supported by research, and it is considered an evidence-based practice in education.

As my class embarks on this journey, I will be keeping you updated about the process through our weekly classroom email newsletter. In addition, I am happy to answer any questions or concerns you may have.

Thank you for supporting your children's learning and growth. I am so thankful to be the teacher of this wonderful class.

Sincerely,

Mrs. Lohmann

From *Positive Behavior Interventions and Supports for Preschool and Kindergarten* by Marla J. Lohmann, © 2021. Published by Redleaf Press, www.redleafpress.org. This page may be reproduced for individual or classroom use only.

APPENDIX E: CLASSROOM SNAPSHOT

NAME OF CHILD	FAMILY STRUCTURE	PERSONALITY AND INTERESTS	NEEDS	BELIEFS (CULTURE/ RELIGION)	OTHER IMPORTANT INFORMATION

From *Positive Behavior Interventions and Supports for Preschool and Kindergarten* by Marla J. Lohmann, © 2021. Published by Redleaf Press, www.redleafpress.org. This page may be reproduced for individual or classroom use only.

APPENDIX F: CHILD PERSONALITY AND INTERESTS ASSESSMENT

NAME OF CHILD:

Preferred Name/Nickname:

Favorites:

Color:

Book:

Game:

Toy:

Movie/TV show:

Food:

Personality traits:

Preferred activities in the classroom:

Preferred activities at home:

Dislikes:

APPENDIX G: PARENT COMMUNICATION LOG

CHILD NAME:			

DATE/TIME	METHOD OF COMMUNICATION	TOPIC OF CONVERSATION	FOLLOW-UP ACTIONS/NOTES

APPENDIX H: CLASSROOM EXPECTATIONS PLANNING DOCUMENT

WHAT I DO NOT WANT CHILDREN TO DO	WHAT I WANT THEM TO DO INSTEAD

APPENDIX I: CLASSROOM EXPECTATIONS MATRIXES

MATRIX FOR THREE CLASSROOM EXPECTATIONS

	EXPECTATION 1	EXPECTATION 2	EXPECTATION 3
Hallways			
Playground			
Bathroom			
Circle Time			
Centers			
Snack/Lunch			
Art			
Table Work			
Rest Time			

MATRIX FOR FOUR CLASSROOM EXPECTATIONS

	EXPECTATION 1	EXPECTATION 2	EXPECTATION 3	EXPECTATION 4
Hallways				
Playground				
Bathroom				
Circle Time				
Centers				
Snack/Lunch				
Art				
Table Work				
Rest Time				

MATRIX FOR FIVE CLASSROOM EXPECTATIONS

	EXPECTATION 1	EXPECTATION 2	EXPECTATION 3	EXPECTATION 4	EXPECTATION 5
Hallways					
Playground					
Bathroom					
Circle Time					
Centers					
Snack/Lunch					
Art					
Table Work					
Rest Time					

DESIGN YOUR OWN MATRIX WITH FIVE CLASSROOM EXPECTATIONS

	EXPECTATION 1	EXPECTATION 2	EXPECTATION 3	EXPECTATION 4	EXPECTATION 5
Hallways					
Playground					
Bathroom					
Circle Time					
Centers					
Snack/Lunch					
Art					
Table Work					
Rest Time					

APPENDIX J: CLASSROOM ROUTINES

TIME OF DAY/ACTIVITY	ROUTINE EXPECTATIONS

APPENDIX K: LESSON REFLECTION

1. What was the topic of my lesson?

2. What was the learning objective?

3. What activities did my lesson include in order to achieve that learning objective?

4. Which children seemed engaged in the lesson?

5. Which children did not seem engaged in the lesson?

6. Were there certain activities that seemed more engaging for children? If so, which ones?

7. Which children met the learning objective?

8. Which children did not meet the learning objective?

9. What went well in the lesson?

10. What did not go well in the lesson?

11. What challenges occurred during the lesson, including behaviors?

12. Which children had behavior challenges?

13. What is my hypothesis for why those particular challenges occurred?

14. What would I do differently if I taught the lesson again?

APPENDIX L: ANTECEDENT-BEHAVIOR-CONSEQUENCE CHART

DATE/TIME/ LOCATION	ANTECEDENT	BEHAVIOR	CONSEQUENCE

APPENDIX M: BEFORE, DURING, AND AFTER THE BEHAVIOR CHART

DATE/TIME/ LOCATION	WHAT HAPPENED BEFORE?	WHAT WAS THE BEHAVIOR?	WHAT HAPPENED AFTER?

APPENDIX N: FREQUENCY RECORDING SHEET—BASIC

DATE	MORNING	AFTERNOON	NOTES

APPENDIX O: FREQUENCY RECORDING SHEET—TIME PERIODS

TIME PERIOD	FREQUENCY OF BEHAVIORS	NOTES
6:00–7:00		
7:00–8:00		
8:00–9:00		
9:00–10:00		
10:00–11:00		
11:00–12:00		
12:00–1:00		
1:00–2:00		
2:00–3:00		
3:00–4:00		
4:00–5:00		
5:00–6:00		
6:00–7:00		

APPENDIX P: FREQUENCY RECORDING SHEET—BLANK

DATE/TIME INTERVAL	FREQUENCY OF BEHAVIORS	NOTES

APPENDIX Q: BEHAVIOR DURATION CHART

DATE	TIME BEHAVIOR STARTED	TIME BEHAVIOR ENDED	TOTAL TIME	NOTES

APPENDIX R: PROCEDURES FOR TIME-OUT FROM AN ACTIVITY

1. Identify the activity/toy/person that is triggering the behavior.

2. Provide two to three reminders of appropriate usage of that item (if physical harm is involved, do not provide reminders).

3. If behavior does not improve, the child loses access to the activity/toy/person for three to five minutes.

4. During the time-out, the child may play with anything else.

5. At the end of three to five minutes, the child receives access to activity/toy/person again.

6. Remind the child of expectations for usage.

7. If behavior with the item is inappropriate again, another time-out occurs.

8. After three time-outs, the child loses access to activity/toy for the day. The child never loses access to a caregiver for the day.

From *Positive Behavior Interventions and Supports for Preschool and Kindergarten* by Marla J. Lohmann, © 2021. Published by Redleaf Press, www.redleafpress.org. This page may be reproduced for individual or classroom use only.

Angela, I like that you are sitting on your spot.

Baya, you are doing a great job of sharing the baby doll.

Chan, thank you for cleaning up the toys.

Danita, thumbs-up for staying in circle time today!

Ellie, high five for writing your letters. I know that it is hard for you.

Francesco, I am proud of you for flushing the toilet without a reminder.

Gabriela, great job of using your inside voice while you play monsters.

Henrik, fantastic work of putting your backpack in your cubby this morning.

Isaiah, excellent work of using your words when José had the car you wanted.

APPENDIX T: PREPARING TO TEACH A REPLACEMENT BEHAVIOR

1. Describe the challenging behavior.

2. Why is this behavior a problem?

3. What is usually the result (consequence: good or bad) of the behavior?

4. What would I like the child to do instead (that still meets the same function)?

5. Why will my desired replacement behavior work better?

6. What are the specific steps of the replacement behavior?

7. What challenges do I foresee in teaching the replacement behavior?

8. What is my plan for teaching the replacement behavior?

APPENDIX U: REWARD MENU

	☺ ☹
	☺ ☹
	☺ ☹
	☺ ☹
	☺ ☹
	☺ ☹
	☺ ☹
	☺ ☹
	☺ ☹
	☺ ☹
	☺ ☹

APPENDIX V: SOCIAL AND EMOTIONAL RESOURCES FOR TEACHERS

RESOURCE	SPECIFIC INFORMATION AVAILABLE
Center on the Social and Emotional Foundations for Early Learning http://csefel.vanderbilt.edu	<ul><li>Overview of the Teaching Pyramid model of preschool PBIS</li><li>Scripted social stories</li><li>Social and emotional lessons based on children's books</li><li>Social and emotional printable teaching tools</li><li>Case studies</li><li>Research briefs</li><li>Articles for families</li></ul>
The National Center for Pyramid Model Innovations http://challengingbehavior.fmhi.usf.edu	<ul><li>Overview of the Teaching Pyramid model of preschool PBIS</li><li>Presentations on implementation</li><li>Articles on implementation</li></ul>
Positive Behavior Interventions and Supports from the OSEP Technical Assistance Center www.pbis.org	<ul><li>Overview of PBIS at all grade levels</li><li>Articles on PBIS at each tier</li><li>Specific information on interventions</li><li>Research briefs</li><li>Articles for teachers and families</li></ul>
#pbischat Weekly Twitter chat on Tuesday evenings at 9:00 EST	<ul><li>Discussions about PBIS implementation in schools</li><li>Sharing of ideas with experts and others who are using PBIS</li></ul>

References

Baillargeon, Raymond H., Claude L. Normand, Jean R. Séguin, Mark Zoccolillo, Christa Japel, Daniel Perusse, Hong-Xing Wu, Michel Boivin, and Richard E. Tremblay. 2007. "The Evolution of Problem and Social Competence Behaviors during Toddlerhood: A Prospective Population-Based Cohort Survey." *Infant Mental Health Journal* 28 (1): 12–38.

Chu, Szu-Yin. 2015. "An Investigation of the Effectiveness of Family-Centered Positive Behavior Support of Young Children with Disabilities." *International Journal of Early Years Education* 23 (2): 172–91.

Gilliam, Walter S. 2014. "What Could Make Less Sense Than Expelling a Preschooler?" *Psychology Benefits Society* (blog), December 13. https://psychologybenefits.org/2014/12/13/preschool -expulsions.

Gilliam, Walter S., and Golan Shahar. 2006. "Preschool and Child Care Expulsion and Suspension Rates and Predictors in One State." *Infants and Young Children* 19 (3): 228–45.

Horner, Robert H., and George Sugai. 2015. "School-Wide PBIS: An Example of Applied Behavior Analysis Implemented at a Scale of Social Importance." *Behavior Analysis in Practice* 8 (1): 80–85.

Jolstead, Krystine A., Paul Caldarella, Blake Hansen, Byran B. Korth, Leslie Williams, and Debra Kamps. 2017. "Implementing Positive Behavior Support in Preschools: An Exploratory Study of CW-FIT Tier 1." *Journal of Positive Behavior Interventions* 19 (1): 48–60.

Joseph, Gail E., and Phillip S. Strain. 2010. "Building Positive Relationships with Young Children." The Center on the Social and Emotional Foundations for Early Learning, Vanderbilt University. http://csefel.vanderbilt.edu/modules/module1/handout5.pdf.

McCloud, Carol. 2006. *Have You Filled a Bucket Today? A Guide to Daily Happiness for Kids.* Northville, MI: Ferne Press.

Meek, Shantel E., and Walter S. Gilliam. 2016. "Expulsion and Suspension in Early Education as Matters of Social Justice and Health Equity." *National Academy of Medicine Perspectives*, discussion paper. https://doi.org/10.31478/201610e.

Nur, Imray, Yaşare Aktaş Arnas, Burcu Sultan Abbak, and Mustafa Kale. 2018. "Mother-Child and Teacher-Child Relationships and Their Associations with School Adjustment in Preschool." *Educational Sciences: Theory and Practice* 18 (1): 201–20. https://doi.org/10.12738/estp.2018 .1.0608.

Peckham-Hardin, Kathryn D. 2002. "Teachers' Reported Use of Positive Behavior Support under Typical Classroom Conditions." Unpublished PhD diss., University of California.

Stanton-Chapman, Tina L., Virginia L. Walker, Mary D. Voorhees, and Martha E. Snell. 2016. "The Evaluation of a Three-Tier Model of Positive Behavior Interventions and Supports for Preschoolers in Head Start." *Remedial and Special Education* 37 (6): 333–44.

Steed, Elizabeth A., Tina Pomerleau, Howard Muscott, and Leigh Rohde. 2013. "Program-Wide Positive Behavioral Interventions and Supports in Rural Preschools." *Rural Special Education Quarterly* 32 (1): 38–46.

Tobin, Tary J., and George Sugai. 2005. "Preventing Problem Behaviors: Primary, Secondary, and Tertiary Level Prevention Interventions for Young Children." *Journal of Early and Intensive Behavior Intervention* 2 (3): 125–44.

Van Craeyevelt, Sanne, Karine Verschueren, Caroline Vancraeyveldt, Sofie Wouters, and Hilde Colpin. 2017. "The Role of Preschool Teacher-Child Interactions in Academic Adjustment: An Intervention Study with Playing-2-gether." *British Journal of Educational Psychology* 87 (3): 345–64. https://doi.org/10.1111/bjep.12153.

Webster-Stratton, Carolyn, and Mary Hammond. 1998. "Conduct Problems and Level of Social Competence in Head Start Children: Prevalence, Pervasiveness, and Associated Risk Factors." *Clinical Child and Family Psychology Review* 1 (2): 101–24.

Weist, Mark D., S. Andrew Garbacz, Kathleen Lynne Lane, and Don Kincaid, eds. 2017. *Aligning and Integrating Family Engagement in Positive Behavioral Interventions and Supports (PBIS): Concepts and Strategies for Families and Schools in Key Contexts*. Center on Positive Behavioral Interventions and Supports (funded by the Office of Special Education Programs, U.S. Department of Education). Eugene: University of Oregon Press.

Williford, Amanda P., Jennifer LoCasale-Crouch, Jessica Vick Whittaker, Jamie DeCoster, Karyn A. Hartz, Lauren M. Carter, Catherine Sanger Wolcott, Bridget E. Hatfield. 2017. "Changing Teacher-Child Dyadic Interactions to Improve Preschool Children's Externalizing Behaviors." *Child Development* 88 (5): 1544–53.

Index

A-B-C (antecedent-behavior-consequence) charts
about, 86
completing, 86–87, 93–94
examples of, 88–89, 91–92
forms, 160–161
understanding, 90, 93
action-research, 30
alternative behaviors, 54
assessments of effectiveness of interventions, 29–30

behavioral challenges
as asking for help, 22
collaboration with families results in fewer, 32
documenting
length of, 101–102, 165
using frequency count, 98–101, 162–164
8:1 rule and sharing with families, 39
family's denial of, 38–39
4:1 rule and sharing with families, 37–38, 39
function of, 85, 118
lesson mismatch with child and, 75, 76–78
lesson not interesting to child, 79–80
planned ignoring of behavior, 118–119
race and gender and, 87
suspension rate for, 2
types of, 1–2
using A-B-C charts to assess, 86–94, 160–161
"wiggly" students, 80–81
worsening of, before improving, 106–107
behavior contracts, 127–129
behaviors
alternative, 54
consequences of, 86
describing, 8
focusing on positive, 22
4:1 rule and sharing with families, 37–38, 39
function of, 85, 118
on-task and off-task behavior studies of PBIS, 10
praising specific, 113–114, 167
of teacher, 72
teaching replacement, 121–123, 125–127, 168, 169

teaching unlearned, 119–120, 125–127, 169
beliefs, 25, 26
best practices
focusing on positive behaviors, 22
respect for each child, 21
bias in classroom, resources for, 87
blocks, 108
breaks, scheduling regular, 124
buckets, filling, 50–51

Center on the Social and Emotional Foundations for Early Learning, 50
challenges, preparing for, 19
Chu, Szu-Yin, 10
Classroom Assessment Scoring System (CLASS), 10
classroom environment
"About Me" posters, 45–46
layout, 17
rules and routines in
being precise about, 55
communicating, 58–59, 61, 69–70
example of, 69
as expectations, 54
lesson plans for, 61–68
listing, 54–58, 153
as matrix of expectations, 59–61, 154–157
planning, 68–69, 159
special morning, 43, 46–47
communication
being precise in, 55
nonverbal clues, 111–112
pre-correction statements, 115
with stakeholders, 17–18, 20, 148
with students
about routines, 69–70, 112–113
about rules, 58–59, 61, 112–113
as chatty and non-questioning, 49
playing, and, 49–50
writing to, 44–45
visual reminders and cues as, 112–113, 124–125
See also communication with *under* families
cues
individualized, 124–125

nonverbal, 111–112
visual, 112–113
culture
nonverbal clues and, 111–112
respect for and learning about each child's, 25,
26–28

documentation
assessment of effectiveness of PBIS, 29–30
behavioral challenges
length of, 101–102, 165
using frequency count, 98–101, 162–164
collection of data, 12–19, 147
of communication with families, 34–35
defining personality and interests of each child,
22, 23–24, 25–26, 150–151
family's denial of behavioral challenges and,
38–39

8:1 rule, 39
emotional needs, 25, 26
evidence-based practices, 29
expectations in classroom
lesson plans for
about, 61–62
reflecting on, 67–68
respecting others in hallways, 62–67
matrix of expectations for, 59–61, 154–157
reasons for children not meeting, 27
rules and routines as, 54

families
barriers to working with, 38–40
behavior interventions and, 37
in classrooms, 38
communication with
about cultural norms, 26
about PBIS, 37, 149
during child's first week in class, 33
continuing, 39–40
documenting, 34–35
homework calendars, 35–36
importance of, 31–32
language barriers and, 40
online video chats, 33
questionnaires sent home to, 22
relationships with students and, 44
visits and, 32
written forms of, 33
8:1 rule and, 39

feelings about their and teacher's expertise,
40–41
4:1 rule and, 37–38, 39
limited available time of, 39
sharing culture with class, 27
structure of, 23, 150
4:1 rule, 37–38, 39

Gilliam, Walter S., 2
Guidelines for Classroom Success, 56–58

Have You Filled a Bucket Today? (McCloud), 50–51
Head Start classrooms study, 10
homework calendars, 35–36
Hunter, Madeline, 120, 121

individualized visual cues, 124–125
interventions for behavioral challenges
choosing appropriate, 97–98
determining efficacy of, 102–103
documentation for, 98–102, 162–165
matching, to specific behavior, 95–97

language barriers, 40
learning goals, 18
lesson plans
for classroom expectations
about, 61–62
reflecting on, 67–68
respecting others in hallways, 62–67
components of Hunter's format, 120
self-reflection on teaching and, 72–75, 159

McCloud, Carol, 50–51
movement, incorporating into lessons, 80–81

nonverbal clues, 111–112

online video chats, 33
on-task behavior studies, 10

parents. *See* families
physical needs, 25, 26
piggy banks, filling, 50–51
playing with students, 49–50
Positive Behavior Interventions and Supports
(PBIS)
assessment effectiveness of, 29–30
basic facts about, 2, 9, 106, 131–132
families and, 37, 149
goal of, 3